BUSHELS OF Nostalgia

by Susan Davis

To: Moose Lake Public Library,

Susan Davis

SGD
PUBLISHING COMPANY

Cover and Book Design by Jim L. Friesen

Library of Congress Catalog Card Number: 2014951503

ISBN: 978-0-692-27425-5

Printed in the United States of America by Mennonite Press, Inc.,
Newton, KS
www.mennonitepress.com

Dedication

To my family, together we collected a "bushel of memories" for us to cherish whenever we choose.

Also, to the communities that surrounded our farm home. They played a vital role in our lives and continue to hold a special place in our hearts.

Introduction

Depending upon the era one grows up in, it makes a huge difference in what type of things or experiences become nostalgic for them later on in life. To me, it's rather remarkable how something ordinary from days gone by can take on a whole new meaning with the passage of years.

I was born in 1952 when housedresses were in style. While Mom cooked three meals a day, she didn't wear a full-length apron over her dress like my grandmother always did. When Dad needed Mom's help out in the field, she changed into a work shirt and a pair of jeans. Eventually, she decided to "hang up" her housedresses for good even though many women were still wearing them. Since she was a dedicated farm wife, she felt like work clothes were the more practical attire for her.

Color photos were still a thing of the future. Our earliest family album contained only black-and-white images of life as we knew it. The pictures were held in place by old-fashioned photo corners that we stuck to the black paper pages.

Six-month-old Susan Davis is pictured in a vintage baby buggy in 1953.

Poodle skirts went out of style before I was old enough to wear one, but those black-and-white Saddle Oxfords were still fashionable. I remember going with Mom to JCPenney and buying a pair of those pretty shoes.

Both of my parents received an education from the same country school that my brothers, sisters and I attended. It was located in the tiny town of Padroni, Colorado. Even though the school was closed years ago, my mind can still picture lively students and familiar teachers' faces from that setting like it was only yesterday. I can recall sitting in a classroom, learning how to read from the Dick and Jane books. The simple, repetitive text went something like this, "Run Dick run. Run Jane run. See Dick run. See Jane run."

The teacher taught our small class the basics of penmanship by utilizing the Palmer Method. We got plenty of practice at drawing overlapping circles as we worked our

Author's Family about 1974

Top row: *Luke, Judy, Susan (also known as Suz by family), Patty, Delores and Tom.*

Bottom row: *Jackie, Mary, Mom holding Dan, Joann and Dad.*

way across the lined paper. We also got proficient at making slightly angled lines side-by-side by using our lead pencils to go up and down between the printed lines. Shortly thereafter, that style of teaching penmanship gave way to new methods.

In later grades, my classmates and I looked forward to getting a Weekly Reader. The four-page educational newspapers contained timely news articles geared to our age level. After reading them, we answered the questions to see how much we had learned.

I was first introduced to short stories in grade school. I thoroughly enjoyed reading them for they were short (like the name implies), sweet and to the point. In a limited number of words, the writer transported the reader to an entirely different setting, introduced the characters and followed through on a theme. I especially liked the stories with a good moral woven into them. My love for that style of writing has continued to present day.

The short stories included in "Bushels of Nostalgia" are based upon events as Dad, Mom and their ten children lived them. Some of the stories not only reflect experiences from the distant past, but they also show how life has progressed through the years. Consequently, it was impossible to put the stories in chronological order.

The book features vintage items and lifestyles from the 50s, 60s and 70s that will have readers recalling their own personal memories from that time period.

By Susan Davis – also author of the books...
Small Farm & Big Family
Ancestry's Journey

Contents

1
Bushel
Baskets of Apples

It was August, and our family was looking forward to the tradition of going apple picking. Late in the afternoon, Mom received the anticipated phone call from Mrs. Hoffman. Their family lived about six miles away, and they had a small orchard. Nearly every summer, they generously gave us as many apples as we wanted free of charge. The only stipulation was we had to pick them ourselves.

Early the next morning, Mom loaded several wooden bushel baskets into our car trunk. For us kids, there was an excitement in the summery air. We were going to be doing something out of the ordinary.

As we pulled into a familiar driveway, I remember thinking how pretty their farmhouse was. It was painted dark brown and trimmed in white. To me, it looked like a chocolate gingerbread house with edges frosted with vanilla icing.

Mom talked briefly with the neighbor lady on the front step. It looked like she had enjoyed their conversation, because she was smiling as she walked back to our car. As she drove west of their house toward the orchard, she said, "Mrs. Hoffman told me it was a really good year for apples."

We soon saw an abundance of ripe fruit dangling from the weighted down tree branches. There were two varieties of apples in the orchard. The small, yellow-skinned ones had a tender, mealy texture. Mom wanted to pick a lot of those, because they cooked down really well and made excellent pies. The small, green apples had a juicy, crisp flesh. They were a good eating apple, one Dad especially liked because of their tartness. We would pick plenty of those, too.

Mrs. Hoffman had informed Mom that we could use the ladder, which was in the orchard. Since Delores was the oldest, she was assigned the job that appeared to be the most fun. She climbed up on the rungs and plucked the apples hanging from the highest branches. She handed them down to her brother Tom, and he put them into the basket. Mom, my younger sisters Patty, Judy and I stood at ground level, reached up as high as we could and picked those. "Don't just throw the apples in the basket!" Mom emphasized. "They bruise easily."

Since we had quite a few pickers, it didn't take us long to fill three bushel baskets to the brim. We carried the heavy baskets by their wire handles, lifted them into the car trunk and headed to our farm.

Just as soon as we got home, my brothers, sisters and I couldn't resist eating our fair share of apples. Meanwhile, Mom set aside the amount she thought we could eat before they spoiled. The rest she would can.

Since we didn't have an air conditioner, our kitchen was hot. To beat the summer heat, Mom, Delores and I set up a workstation under our three rows of elm trees. They would provide shade while we prepared the apples for canning.

The first step was to put the fruit in a large, galvanized tub, fill it with cool water and wash the bobbing apples. Next, we started the tedious, time-consuming task of splitting the tiny apples into quarters, removing the cores and stems and slicing them into bite-size pieces. Mom told us there was no need to peel the tender-skinned round beauties. However, she did instruct us to cut away any spots where worms had been feasting on the tasty fruit.

The ground became our wastebasket. Every summer I hoped that several of the brown seeds, which dropped to the soil would sprout, grow tall and someday produce apples in our yard, but that never happened. One of the reasons might have been our hungry, free-range chickens. Once the appealing food source was discovered, the entire flock ventured over. We tossed them some of the discarded portions of the apples, and they eagerly pecked away, cleaning up the seeds and all.

When we had enough sliced apples for Mom to start the canning process, she carried the full bowl inside. Delores and I continued to whittle away at the remaining apples. The birds were singing in the tree branches high above us. Their rhythmic songs were so cheerful it made working outdoors almost a pleasure. It certainly was more fun than being inside in the hot kitchen.

After awhile, my hands got tired from maneuvering the knife and from gripping the apples, but I kept on cutting. Meanwhile, my mind had a chance to drift away. I remembered Dad telling me that he had helped his parents plant the shade trees when he was a boy. Being under them was the coolest place on our farm. Many times when we got company on Sunday afternoons in the summertime, Mom suggested, "Let's go outside. It's too hot in here." Each of the adults grabbed a kitchen chair, walked across our graveled farmyard and headed for our shade trees. While the grown-ups relished a leisurely visit and a glass of tart lemonade, the kids frolicked beneath the roof created by those elm trees.

Coming back to reality, I noticed the end was in sight. Only about half a bushel of whole apples remained to be cut up. Once the slicing was finished, we carried the big bowls filled with the pieces of fruit inside. Mom was still busy as a bee in the stuffy kitchen doing the canning.

By mid-afternoon, our combined efforts had yielded many quarts of cooked apples. When Mom knew all of the jars had sealed properly and were cool enough to carry, she asked Patty and Judy to take them down to our cool cellar. There they would be stored on shelves until she decided to bake a couple of tasty apple pies for her family.

Once again, the bushel baskets were stored away in hopes of a good apple crop next summer. It had been a tiring day but one well spent.

2
Drive-In Theater

The Starlite Drive-In Theater, located a few miles west of Sterling, Colorado, was opened in 1950 during the height of the outdoor movie trend. The owner had purchased ten acres of land, designed a facility that held up to 500 cars and erected two movie screens.

By the summer of 1954, it wasn't just a popular entertainment spot to watch a movie after dark. The Methodist church began holding an early morning service at the location. The choir and minister were stationed up on the concession stand roof, and the music and sermon were broadcast through portable car speakers. On an average Sunday, more than 50 carloads of people started their day off at this unconventional place of worship.

As a young child, I only remember going to the drive-in one time with my parents. Dad liked westerns and one was playing. He stopped at a little booth and paid the attendant the admission fee. When we went around the corner, I saw long rows of poles spaced a little more than a car width apart. Each pole had two speakers hanging from it.

Dad picked a parking spot and drove the front wheels of our car up on a small embankment. Delores, Tom and I were sitting in the back seat of the vehicle, and it seemed very strange having the front end of the automobile angled up higher than the back of it. It was impossible to miss the huge, blank screen that was visible through the front windshield of our car. "Why isn't there anything for us to watch?" I asked.

"Because it's not dark enough for them to start playing the movie, yet," Mom explained. Like typical kids, we quickly grew restless waiting for something to happen.

When the screen finally lit up, Dad rolled his window down partway, grabbed the speaker on his side and hooked it onto the window. He turned the knob, and we heard the actors' scratchy voices enter our car. I could hardly believe my ears and my eyes! The vibrant color made the cowboys and horses look real, and they were huge. I'd never seen anything like it before.

For quite awhile, the motion picture captured my attention. When I felt sleepy, I crawled up on the package shelf by the back window. Thus, my early childhood memory of watching a movie in the great outdoors ended before the western did.

A couple of decades later, the drive-in was still a popular warm weather attraction. On pleasant evenings, a few people brought lawn chairs with them, and they enjoyed the movie under a starry sky. Others preferred viewing it from the privacy and comfort of their vehicles. It was always tempting for patrons to turn around and watch the screen behind them at least for a brief period of time. The only problem was they could see the action, but there was no sound to accompany it.

At intermission, a popcorn advertisement "popped up" on the big screen. It made the snack look irresistible. Smart moviegoers made sure they knew where their car was parked before leaving it. If they didn't, it wasn't easy to find their vehicle among all the others in the dark. Upon entering the concession stand, a wonderful smell greeted customers. Bars guided them through the waiting area to where popcorn, pop and candy could be purchased.

People munched on their snacks while the second half of the movie played. If the thin film happened to break, the screen went blank and the sound went silent. That is until lots of car horns began honking. This most certainly alerted the person in charge of the projection booth to repair the film.

Another circumstance that made drivers honk their horns was when someone rudely left their bright, distracting dome light on too long. They soon got the message and shut it off. It was also an unwritten rule that if you wanted to leave early, you drove out of the lot with just your park lights on.

When the movie officially ended, viewers slowly drove through the exit across metal bars that sounded like vehicles going over a cattle guard. The owner of the business had installed them so people couldn't enter in through the exit and watch the motion picture for free. As the cars left the drive-in, one after another, there soon became a steady stream of vehicles traveling down West Main. It looked like rush hour around midnight.

Years ago, patrons of drive-in theaters didn't have a clue that they would slowly fizzle away. Today, they have almost totally disappeared from the American scene. They were usually located on the outskirts of a town. When the city limits expanded, the land was often sold for more profitable purposes.

During the decades when drive-ins were popular, moviegoers could also go on a date to the "show" at the downtown theater. It offered an indoor setting to viewers. Back in the day, when my husband and I were dating, he'd ask, "Do you want to go to the drive-in or to the show?" At least in the warm months of the year, we had two different choices of entertainment sites.

We're now part of the older generation. Today, we still slip up and say that we're going to the show. Our grown kids laugh and quickly exclaim, "You're going to the movies!"

Must be that generation gap!

3
Black-
and-White
Television

Mom and Dad weren't the kind of people who rushed right out and bought new items on the market. They let other people try them out first, and then decided if it was something they truly needed or wanted.

The year was 1958 when they finally decided to purchase a black-and-white television. It was a tabletop model manufactured by Zenith. They also bought a gold metal stand to sit it on. Although this probably was a big event at our household, I don't remember being thrilled about getting a TV. I had watched them at my grandparents' homes; consequently, they weren't foreign to me.

Dad had to put up an antenna in order for us to get reception. First, he dug a deep hole in the ground near the south side of our farmhouse. A utility pole was hoisted into place and tapped into the ground. The pole was slightly taller than the peak of our roof. He attached a metal pipe, which ran parallel to it. Finally, he installed the antenna at the top of the pipe.

When the television was turned on, the reception was all snowy. The large picture window in the living room was opened, allowing my parents to communicate through it. Dad turned the pipe that controlled the direction the antenna was pointed. Meanwhile, Mom informed him if he was making the picture and sound better or worse. Once they got the antenna adjusted, we were able to pick up three local channels, which also happened to be the major networks in the country – CBS, NBC and ABC.

The black-and-white television certainly never came with a remote control. To turn the TV on, we pulled out a knob that our family called a "button." To change channels, we turned the numbered dial.

Before long, the television became the center of our family's entertainment. We felt like we got acquainted with the folks who lived in the quaint town of Mayberry. We also thoroughly enjoyed stopping by the sprawling Ponderosa Ranch to follow the adventures of the Cartwrights.

We soon reached the point where we knew what day of the week it was simply by what programs were on. Years later, it isn't hard to recall that Lassie was broadcast at five o'clock Mountain Standard Time on Sunday evening, followed by The Ed Sullivan Show. Saturday night wasn't just our weekly bath night; it was also time to tune into The Lawrence Welk Show and Gunsmoke.

There were times when our television quit working. It didn't do any good to go outside and adjust the antenna. Dad figured it was probably the picture tube. He hauled it into Sterling to the repair shop where it usually took several days to get fixed. Without a small screen to watch, there wasn't much to do in the evenings. We were glad when Dad drove into town to pick it up. Life got back to normal once the television set was in its designated place.

Sometimes regular programming was interrupted, because the network was conducting a test. All of a sudden, the screen got snowy and a shrill-pitched noise blared. A prerecorded voice would come on and say, "This is only a test. If this had been an actual emergency, you would have been instructed to seek shelter." The interruption in regular programming never lasted long, but the message always scared me a little. It reinforced the fact that the U.S. was in a Cold War with Russia.

At that time, we were also in a race with the Russians to see who could get to the moon first. Whenever a spacecraft was going to be launched into outer space, the event was covered on TV. The weather could cause the launch to be delayed or cancelled for a later date. If all conditions were right, the newsman built up the scene, "Ten, nine, eight, seven, six, five, four, three, two, one…we have lift off!" Smoke billowed, and the rocket slowly shot upward. Like the rest of the country, we wondered if everything would go according to plan. When the mission had been completed and the capsule was about to land in the ocean, regular programming was interrupted to show the astronauts arriving safely back at earth.

Another country changing event that my family gathered around our black-and-white screen to watch happened on November 22, 1963. All major networks were telecasting the shocking news that President Kennedy was shot in Dallas. We absorbed the details as they unfolded in disbelief.

Eventually, my parents followed the trend and bought a colored TV, which was a console model. We were hooked immediately and had no desire to go back to the black-and-white version.

When our family of 12 gathered around the television, the living room seemed to shrink in size. All of my siblings and I liked to sit in one particular chair. We considered it the best seat in the house. Jackie only left the room for a minute; but by the time she came back, Mary had run over and joined Joann on the chair. Two of the younger kids could easily fit into the soft, cushiony space. Reluctantly, Jackie sat down on the couch beside her brother Luke. She was just waiting for him to pick on her like he loved to do.

During the daytime, my brothers, sisters and I definitely didn't overextend our privilege of watching TV. That's because we were usually kept busy working around the farm. The television wasn't left on just to provide background noise. If Mom noticed no one was watching it, she either hastily turned it off herself or she asked the person near it to do so. This time, it happened to be Dan. "Shut that thing off!" she exclaimed. She preferred peace and quiet, something she rarely got with ten kids.

The radio was a different means of communication that my parents had grown up with. They liked to listen to it early in the morning around breakfast time and at noon. Our light brown, plastic radio sat on our kitchen countertop in the corner. Since there was no picture to convey a message, it helped if a good voice projected out of it.

Mom paid close attention to the local hospital report. She was interested in finding out who had been recently admitted or dismissed from the hospital. Dad could have cared less about that report, but he anxiously listened to the weather forecast. Actually, both my parents usually stopped what they were doing and stood around the radio absorbing Weatherman Bowman's predictions.

And just like the television set, the radio dial was turned off if no one was listening to it.

4
Icehouse

Before our family bought a deep freezer in 1959, we stored our farm raised, home butchered meats in a locker at Sterling Ice and Cold Storage Company. They charged a $60 per year rental fee. The icehouse was "housed" in a large brick building alongside Cudahy Packing Company. The two businesses worked in conjunction with one another.

For the customers' convenience, the storage facility was open 24 hours per day. We generally only stopped by our locker once a week, which was usually on Sunday mornings after attending church. Mom picked up the frozen foods she would need for the upcoming week's meals. The freezer portion of our refrigerator was large enough to hold that much food.

How I remember those hot summer days when I tagged along with Mom inside the unique business. There was a huge temperature change between the sunny outdoors and what seemed like the frozen tundra. It was bone chilling, and goose bumps quickly covered my exposed skin. The frigid air had a subtle odor to it, similar to digging inside a home freezer these days.

We trudged up a steep ramp, went through swinging doors and wound our way through dimly lit passageways that were bordered by lockers stacked upon each other. The corridors felt like we were walking down a tunnel. Our voices echoed as we talked. Upon arriving at our rented space, my mother dug the key out of her purse. Our storage area was located on the bottom row. The metal door rattled as she opened it. The locker was approximately three feet wide by three feet high. It was deep enough to accommodate about 300 pounds of food. When our locker was packed, it was hard for her to find exactly what she wanted.

Pork was the predominant meat stored in our cubbyhole. By midsummer, Mom began butchering the roosters she raised. Packages of them would be stockpiled in our town freezer. She typically brought one home to cook for Sunday dinner. We also grew blackberries in our garden. Bags of the frozen fruit would be kept in our "mini warehouse" at the storage facility until Mom decided she wanted to make them into pie, dumplings or jelly.

When the pork supply ran low, Dad and Mom would home butcher another hog that we raised. The weather conditions had to be right in order to keep the meat from spoiling. They typically butchered in the late afternoon when it was cold outdoors. The carcass was hung from a strong tree branch or in the barn overnight.

The next morning, my parents cut up the meat into roasts and pork chops. The rest of it was going to be made into sausage. They carefully trimmed away all the scraps they could from the soup bones so nothing was wasted. Then they rushed into town with the heavy load.

Cudahy Packing Company wrapped the roasts and

chops, charging by the pound. As a customer service, they would sharp freeze the labeled packages before putting them into our locker. My parents waited as an employee ground up the remainder of their pork into a sausage grind. They also purchased casings from the business.

Dad and Mom hurriedly left the facility with the ground pork and casings. They were anxious to get home and begin preparing a big batch of German sausage. Since they were out of their farm-raised beef and they needed to combine it with the pork, they still had to stop over at the grocery store and purchase some hamburger.

Back at the farm, Dad mixed equal amounts of the two meats together in a large tub along with garlic, salt and pepper. Mom fried a small patty of German sausage, so they could do a taste test. When they were satisfied that the meat was properly seasoned, it was run through a sausage stuffer and forced into pieces of casing, forming rings. Once this process was finished, they once again drove into town. It was a lot of running back and forth, but there was no other way they could do it.

My parents watched as an employee from the packing company wrapped each ring of sausage in a clear wrapping and then in a white, heavy-duty freezer paper. The bill was figured up, and they paid the amount owed. They trusted the facility to sharp freeze the labeled packages of sausage and stack them into their locker.

Dad told me that he remembers the time when Sterling Ice and Cold Storage also sold blocks of ice. Individuals who relied solely upon iceboxes for all of their refrigeration needs gladly purchased it. As time went on and refrigerators became a common appliance in kitchens, the necessity for that service became obsolete.

Unfortunately, another change was on the horizon for the long-standing business. When others like my parents purchased their own deep freezers, the need for a local ice-house melted away. A couple of new inventions had "iced" its fate.

5
The Cold Room

During the 25 years that we rented the small farm, our landlord did two major remodels on the house. The first one was completed when I was six-years-old. I remember a bathroom and second porch were added on. Mom was thrilled about finally having running water just a faucet away.

While that remodel had made big improvements, our home still had its share of drawbacks. The only sources of heat that we had was a propane stove located in the living room and a diesel stove was in my parents' bedroom. The two stovepipes were routed so that the fumes went out the same chimney. Every room in our home had high ceilings; and since heat just naturally likes to rise, it was hard to keep the place warm.

Typically, snowstorms and stiff winter winds attack from the north. The girls' bedroom was located on the northwest corner of the house right beside Mom and Dad's bedroom.

Consequently, the heat from the diesel stove had to travel through the connecting doorway, which didn't work very well. Fittingly, our family referred to that portion of the house as the "Cold Room."

On bitterly cold nights, my sisters and I never wasted any time getting ready for bed. The linoleum floor felt icy to our bare feet. We quickly crawled under a heavy, home-made quilt that kept us quite cozy.

The Cold Room was also where Mom kept her treadle sewing machine. It was made by the White Company. It had originally belonged to her mother, but it still worked very well. While the machine was mostly black, it did have some pretty gold designs and a few bouquets of flowers decorating it. I remember Mom rocking the black treadle back and forth with both feet. That action spun a large wheel on the treadle frame. A leather belt connected it to a smaller driving wheel on the sewing machine. As the needle stitched away, Mom's hands were kept just as busy as her feet. When she wasn't sewing, the machine was tucked inside a brown wood cabinet. It had three small drawers on each side where she kept her supplies.

Mom used the treadle sewing machine to make the heavy quilts for all of our beds. The time-consuming part of quilt making was stitching old scraps of thick, durable material together. She sewed them in a patchwork style to form the top cover. She purchased flannel for the backing and stitched the two sides and one end together. Next, she put a fluffy layer of batting between the two pieces of material and hand tied segments of heavy string at intervals to hold it in place. Finally, she hemmed the last open end of the quilt.

Of course, when a quilt got dirty, it had to be washed. Us girls got the fun job of taking it apart. Delores sat on the floor and snipped the knotted threads with scissors. I pulled them out and tossed the old strings into a wastebasket. It took us a little longer to unravel the hemmed end. We then rolled back the cover and carefully removed the white batting, because only the shell of the quilt could be washed.

After it was clean, our living room floor became an assembly area. The cover was turned inside out, laid flat and a layer of batting spread over it. The next step took several of us to roll it right side out and keep the filling smooth and even. Mom was then ready to hand tie the three layers together and hem the open end.

During the warmer months of the year, the quilts were stored away and lighter blankets covered the beds. Then, the Cold Room became a wonderful place for my sisters and me to play. Since the bedroom was located in the north forty, we felt like we had plenty of privacy. One of our favorite things to play was dress up. There was an antique trunk in our closet that was filled with old clothes that were way too big for us. It was also where our mother's satiny wedding gown was stored. We had permission to try on anything we wanted to, except her wedding dress. We followed her rule completely, because we already sensed the value of the keepsake.

However, the days of playing in the Cold Room were numbered. I was in fifth grade when our landlord decided to do the second major remodel. Existing doorways between rooms were filled in and new entryways were constructed. The old-fashioned windows were replaced with more contemporary ones. A hallway was added between two of the bedrooms and larger closets were built. The wallpapered rooms were paneled and new floor tile installed. Mom was grateful that the living room ceiling was lowered. I remember when the carpenters weren't around, she remarked, "I don't know why they would ever build houses with such high ceilings in the first place."

Dad discarded the old propane and diesel stoves, for they had done served their purpose. Mom was thrilled to be rid of the mess they made. A modern heating system was installed, which warmed the house evenly.

Perhaps an unexpected change came out of the remodel when the boys and girls switched bedrooms. While the bedroom on the northwest corner of the house had been known for years as the Cold Room, the nickname no longer fit. It had lost that distinction. We began referring to it as the boys' bedroom, since that is where Tom, Luke and Dan now slept.

The antique trunk filled with old clothes was moved over to the beet labor shack. Before doing so, Mom removed her wedding gown and stored it safely away. At first it seemed strange not to play dress up in the Cold Room, but before long the shack began to feel like a used clothing store. My sisters Delores, Patty, Judy, Mary, Jackie, Joann and I had fun trying on the wrinkled garments. We certainly didn't have any designer outfits to model, but we did weave together some warm childhood memories in the process.

6
Tin Can Weather Caps

For most of the years that Dad and Mom farmed, they never had a machine shed in which to store their farm equipment in. Therefore, Dad did the next best thing. He parked our tractors, trucks, combine and farm implements in various locations under the many shade trees, which surrounded our yard. The trees offered some natural shelter from the weather elements.

Still, that wasn't enough protection. Dad chose to cover the exhaust pipes of our tractors with tin cans, because it was the cheapest method of keeping them from rusting out and from water getting into the engine. His logical explanation for this was, "We ate pork and beans most every day and those cans were just about the right size to fit over the pipe. So why buy weather caps?" Of course, if a can was too large, it never worked very well. A strong gust of wind could blow it off.

As I look back now, I realize it was our unintentional way

of recycling. If we needed a new weather cap, we simply saved an empty can, peeled off the label and washed out the inside of it. Soon, we had a shiny, silver one adorning the top of an exhaust pipe.

Whenever Dad was ready to take a tractor out to the field, he usually remembered to remove the can. If he didn't, it would pop off and go flying, landing who knows where. After he came back in from the field, he parked the tractor in its usual spot under the trees. He generally slipped the can over the pipe while it was still hot, because it was the best way to remember to do so. Of course, there was the possibility that he might be in too big of a hurry or have his mind elsewhere and forget to put the protective can on.

I recall one late afternoon when the sky turned dark. It was easy to tell that a rainstorm was quickly approaching. Dad had gotten in from the field moments earlier, but he must have had his doubts whether he had covered the exhaust pipe of his tractor or not. He told my brother Luke, "Run out and make sure that I didn't forget to put the can on our 60."

When Luke came back into the house, his shirt showed a few signs of wet raindrops soaking into it. He reported that the tin can was indeed in place. "Better to be safe than sorry," Dad had replied.

It took a little extra effort to use tin cans as weather caps, but Dad never seemed to mind one bit. When his farming career began in 1950, he had to hitch up a team of workhorses before he went to the field. Shortly thereafter, he acquired a used John Deere, and it probably seemed like a luxury to him. While some farmers had umbrellas on their tractors to provide shade, Dad just wore a straw hat. He never had a tractor with a cab on it until the early 70s. He just made do with what he had.

While opening up a can of pork and beans recently, I

thought about how Dad had used them as a substitute for weather caps. For the first time in my life, I began to wonder if it was unique just to our family. Out of curiosity, I struck up a conversation with a man who had also grown up on a small farm and was about my age. I told him briefly about how my family had used tin cans as weather caps.

I could tell by the smile that warmed his face he had some similar memories. He casually leaned back in his chair as he proceeded to share them with me, "We owned a John Deere D. It had a larger exhaust pipe than most John Deere tractors had. We used Hi-C juice cans to cover it." He grinned before adding, "Our combine had a cone-shaped exhaust pipe with holes in it. We used an old milk bucket to keep it covered."

Not expecting that answer, I laughed before saying, "Guess farmers will use almost anything as long as it works."

With that, our conversation ended. Both of us had enjoyed taking a few minutes out of our current day to "recycle" stories about cheap weather caps.

7
Home Permanents and Clippers

Our kitchen often served as a makeshift beauty salon/
barbershop. Mom was the only one who worked
there and her customer base was simply her husband and ten kids. Since this was just one of her side jobs
as a housewife and mother, I'm sure she kept busy enough
with that many clients.

Although she had no professional training to be a beau-
tician, she gave her girls haircuts and perms. Like many
other women across the country, she bought the popular,
well-advertised Toni home permanent kits. She opted to do
this, because it was a lot cheaper to do-it-yourself than go
to a professional.

In the late 50s and early 60s, I remember a typical perm
day at our household going something like this: Dad had
left in the morning to attend a farm sale, and he wouldn't

be back until late in the afternoon. Mom mentioned that it would be the perfect time to give Patty a permanent, because he wouldn't be home for dinner. She could prepare something easier than usual and at a convenient time.

Mom got busy setting up her "salon" on the kitchen table. She didn't have a fancy beauty shop sink with a spray nozzle to wash Patty's hair in, so she simply filled a large metal bowl with warm water. She shampooed her third oldest daughter's hair and rinsed it by pouring water over her head from a smaller bowl.

After giving her a haircut with a sharp pair of scissors, Mom divided her dishwater blonde locks into sections. She was then ready to begin rolling. She combed a tiny portion of hair straight up. With her other hand, she folded a piece of end wrap around it, which looked like tissue paper. She was careful to position it just beyond the ends of the strands. She wrapped the length of the hair smoothly and evenly over the perm rod before fastening it. This procedure was repeated until all of her hair was rolled up.

Mom then wrapped a long strip of cotton around Patty's hairline and handed her a towel. "Wipe any drips with this," she instructed. "Don't let it get into your eyes." As she applied the waving lotion on each rod, a chemical smell immediately filled the kitchen.

It didn't take Patty long to complain, "It's making my eyes and nose burn." The rest of us in the house understood why she was grumbling. The odor was overpowering. She left the strong solution on according to the directions on the box, which was 20 minutes. When the processing time was up, Mom partially unrolled a rod to check for waviness. She was satisfied with the amount of curl, so she wrapped it back up and thoroughly rinsed Patty's head with warm water.

After dabbing the excess moisture off the rods with a dry towel, she began applying the neutralizer. The box directions were to leave it on for five minutes. After that length of time, she removed the perm rods and end wraps. She waited another five minutes before rinsing Patty's hair a final time. Since we never had a hair dryer, her newly acquired curls were allowed to air dry.

While Mom didn't mind giving her girls home permanents, she didn't feel comfortable giving herself one. Her sister Rose had agreed to give her a permanent, but they'd have to wait for an opportune time to do so. That happened when Dad decided to attend Cheyenne Frontier Days, freeing her up from cooking for him. Mom thought it would be a good time to take the day off and do something different. My siblings and I went along to Aunt Rose's house, which was about an hour away.

While the two ladies enjoyed visiting and beautifying, my brothers, sisters and I had fun playing outdoors with our cousins. I'm sure our mothers were glad that we were "out of their hair" even though it was only for a short while.

On the drive back to our farm, the distinctive scent of perm filled the car. It was amazing how a product in a box could make Mom's hair much curlier than it had been only a few hours before. However, she realized the new hairdo wouldn't be permanent. In about four months, she'd need to get another home perm.

The day also quickly arrived when it was time for Mom to get the clippers out and turn her kitchen in a barbershop again. It didn't matter the age of the males in our household, they all got crew cuts. Once she was finished, their hair would be the same bristly length on the top, sides and back.

It was Luke's turn to get buzzed. Her second oldest son sat down on a kitchen chair. The clippers made quite a racket, but it didn't take her long to finish cutting his hair. "Next," she said, looking at Dad. He took his seat. After the clippers bogged down, she said, "You've got really thick hair. It almost looks like bear hair."

Caring for her family's hair was an ongoing task for Mom. Perhaps, that is why she came up with the following theory – cut it short, the shorter the better. My youngest sister, Joann, remembers getting those kinds of haircuts, wishing it could be longer. And my oldest brother, Tom, really didn't like getting crew cuts all the time, but he didn't get a choice in the matter.

Mom's way of thinking worked. It allowed her to "lengthen" the time out before she'd have to turn her kitchen into a makeshift beauty salon/barbershop again.

8
Dried Fish

Years ago, drying foods was a common way of preserving them. I recall my parents used the dehydration method several times when they got an abundance of fish.

The day when Dad and our neighbor Glen pulled into the yard with a big washtub full of orange-colored carp is still clear in my mind. They told us that the main gate at the reservoir had been shut off temporarily. There wasn't much water left in the outlet ditch, and a lot of small to medium-size carp were swimming around in it. They thought the other fishermen on the bank were kind of foolish when they commented, "Who wants carp? They're not good for anything." Dad and Glen had different ideas, though. They'd make some delicious dried fish.

After dividing them up evenly, Glen headed for home and my parents got busy. Dad cleaned the carp and cut the larger fillets into smaller strips. Mom sprinkled salt onto the pieces of fish and rubbed it into them. She used a knife to make a small hole near the end of each portion. She threaded binder twine through the holes and strung the fish together in groups before hanging them out on the clothesline. Pesky flies didn't bother the smelly carp much, because they didn't like the salt. As an added precaution, she wrapped a piece of sheer material around them to keep the flies from landing directly on them.

Both the sun and wind contributed to the preservation process. Typically, it took around ten days to two weeks for the thickest portions of the carp to be cured. When they became light colored and were dry as a board, it was time to take the fillets off of the twine. Before long, everyone was enjoying a piece of dried fish. We tore off leathery chunks with our teeth or ripped a section off with our hands. As we chewed, it became flavorful and softer, similar to beef jerky.

One summer, Mom decided to try hanging a batch of salted fish up in our beet labor shack. It was very hot in the small building, but there wasn't any wind to help dry the fillets. It was taking longer than usual for the curing process to happen. My siblings and I made a lot of trips over to the shack to see if we could start feasting on the fish. Finally, Delores grew impatient. She began sampling on the driest edges before the entire fillet was bone dry. Judy decided to join her by tearing off a small piece as well. Like a chain reaction, the rest of us were soon snacking, too.

Another time, Dad caught around 100 small suckers in the shallow South Platte River, which was located a few miles away from our farm. The weather was too cold to hang the cleaned fish outdoors. He hung strings of the salted fillets above the propane furnace in our living room. It wasn't the most decorative sight in the world, but again us kids could hardly wait for them to cure. The dried fish tasted like a delicacy and were quickly gone.

I recall another instance when Dad took his older kids fishing at the South Platte River. We sat on the bank for hours, and it became obvious that the fish weren't hungry. It was rather boring, because they weren't even nibbling on our bait. All of a sudden, my homemade pole, which was made from a tree branch, alerted me differently. Yanking a fish clear out of the shallow water, I yelled, "I caught one!" After Dad took if off the hook for me, it was time for us to head for home. I was rather disappointed, since the fun had just started.

As we were walking back to the car, I casually flipped my pole over my shoulder and to my dismay it hooked my sweatshirt. Try as I might, the barbed hook remained buried in the material. I really didn't want to tell Dad. My thinking was that he'd never take us kids fishing again, because we were too much trouble. After all, we couldn't bait our hooks, take the fish off and I carelessly hooked my clothes.

Dad didn't go fishing very often, but for some odd reason it seemed like we had dried fish on quite a few occasions. One time, his oldest brother, John, who had made a career out of the army, was home for good. He came out to our farm to visit. Us kids hardly knew our uncle, because he'd been in the military for 20 years. We were intrigued with how stiff and formal his actions were until Dad offered him some dried fish. As he was chewing on a piece, he started relaxing and talking about how much he'd enjoyed the snack as a farm boy. It was easy to tell that a wonderful "preserved memory" had been tapped upon.

Dad later told me that his parents had used a little different preparation method than Mom did. They soaked the fillets in a brine solution. If an egg floated in the water, it had enough salt in it. If not, they added some more. "It doesn't make a nickel's worth of difference how it's done, they turn out about the same," he had informed me.

While many people have never tasted fish dried the old-fashioned way, it was a treat two generations in a row got to experience at our farm.

9
A Wood Windmill

The wood windmill that I remember on our small farm wasn't located in either of our two pastures. Instead it loomed high above the corral, which was adjacent to the southern edge of our yard. While the strong wood framework had stood the test of time, the curved steel blades were missing, making it no longer functional.

There were plenty of days when my siblings and I decided to scale our way up the old tower and roost near the top of it. It was a challenge, but that was part of the fun. We climbed the corral fence and pulled ourselves up on the brooder house roof. It was then easy to step over onto the windmill's frame. The wood had become gray and split with age, making us realize it was indeed an antique. As we maneuvered our way upward, splinters occasionally become embedded in our hands. Still, the adventure out-weighed any pain we endured.

We liked to find a comfortable place on the windmill to perch. I remember when a lovely, yellow-breasted meadowlark nested in the tree nearby. It felt great to be as high as a bird. She relied upon her wings to keep her safe; we trusted our agility to prevent us from falling and getting seriously hurt. If Mom and Dad were concerned about our safety, they never expressed it.

We could look down and see our galvanized stock tank that was about 20 yards away from the windmill. It was located near our pump house. In the winter months, the cattle were penned up in the corral, and we used a hose to fill up the tank. Sometimes during the warmer months of the year, the big ditch flowing through one of our pastures became dry. Once again, we relied upon our well to provide them with needed water.

The farm animals didn't care if the water they drank came from an energy efficient windmill or from a well whose electric pump clicked away kilowatts on a meter. It mattered to my parents, though, who had to pay for the pumping of water. In those days, the electric company sent out postcards and trusted us to fill in the current meter reading. After writing in the figure, we put the prepaid postcard into the mailbox. It was returned to them, so they could bill us.

I have fond memories of a few hot summer days when the stock tank became a unique place for my brothers, sisters and me to cool off. We only filled the tank up partway, because none of us could swim. Still, we had fun wading around in it and splashing one another. We were glad that the cattle were busy grazing in the pasture, so they never came by our "swimming pool" for a drink. Can you imagine what they would have thought about a bunch of rowdy kids playing in their tank?

Since our windmill hadn't served a useful purpose for years, it was eventually torn down before it collapsed on its own accord. For our family, the only reminders of it are a few black-and-white pictures. The intriguing piece of farming history just happened to be captured in the background of those snapshots.

But in its heyday, the windmill had played an important role around the farm. When the wind was cooperating, the pump rod made the distinctive sound of chink...chink as it went up and down repeatedly. With each change of wind direction, the blades had no choice but to spin accordingly. Every once in a while, the stately fixture moaned and creaked as if to say, "This is work pumping water from hundreds of feet below the surface! Won't you please change my gear oil?"

While windmills may be endangered, they aren't extinct. There are still remote places where electric power isn't readily available. Even in modern times, they are needed to harness the natural resource of the wind and efficiently pump water for livestock grazing on the open rangeland.

For most windmills, though, their working years are behind them. If no one has bothered to tear them down, they remain intact. Photographers can't resist stopping to snap scenic pictures of them, because they are photogenic. But more than that, those old windmills tell the history of settlers depending upon them to survive the harsh elements of the sunbaked plains.

10
Corn Broom and Waxing Floors

With 24 feet tracking dirt into our house, Mom needed to sweep our floors every day. She was probably convinced that our shoes were like magnets. They attracted all sorts of farm grime while they were stomping around outdoors. It was just a given dilemma, living in the country.

Generally, we marched straight into the house without wiping off our shoes. If it was wet outdoors, we did stop briefly to use a rusty scraper that was built into the edge of one of our front steps. It got rid of most of the mud.

Once inside, our shoes did a good job of cleaning themselves. Particles of mud, which were buried in the crevices of the soles, broke away and littered the floor. It didn't take Mom long to ask, "Who's got mud on their shoes?" Everyone quickly checked the bottoms of their shoes and hoped they were clean. For the guilty party, it was a certain trip back outdoors to dig the mud out of the grooves with a stick.

It was Mom's routine to sweep every room of our home with a corn broom that had a long, yellow wooden handle. Its bristles were tightly banded together. Invariably, the kitchen seemed to attract the most dirt. There were bits and pieces of food dropped under the table during meals. It didn't take her long to accumulate a pile of debris in the center of the floor.

Mom really got involved with her housework whenever she swept our two front cement steps. She vigorously swung the broom from side to side, causing a pleasant swish... swishing sound. If some mud had dried on the cement surface, she utilized the end of her broomstick to loosen it. She then swept the dirt off the step. It blew clear of the area she was cleaning and landed on the ground nearby. She could only hope it would stay there permanently. After finishing her task, she liked to pause for a minute or two and soak up some warm sunshine. The brightness of the sun often caused her to sneeze several times before she headed back inside with her broom in hand.

The tile floor in the living room was old, and it had a distinctive pattern. Every other square was dark red with thin streaks of black running through it. The tile right beside it was tannish-green and stripes of various shades broke up the main color. Mom told me that Dad had chosen the combination. She didn't exactly love it, but she was pleased that the floor wore well. The only problem was it didn't have a no-wax finish. She scrubbed the tile floor every week on her hands and knees but didn't always take the time to wax it. When she did, she again got down on the floor and used a rag to apply a paste wax, which came in a round can. It went on dull and was strong smelling.

Once Mom had worked her way across the living room, it was time for us girls to help. She rummaged through her rag pile for enough small, soft cloths for everyone. Like her, we got down on our hands and knees and used the rags to rub over the waxy surface. It soon became slick and shiny.

After we had polished the entire floor, my dark-haired sister Judy stood up and slid across the slippery surface on her socked feet. She looked as graceful as a skater gliding on ice at a rink. Before long, the rest of us couldn't resist taking off our shoes and joining her. When we were finished playing, the tiles looked very pretty.

Mom cared for her living room floor in this manner for almost two decades. Finally, my parents broke down and bought a carpet for that room. For the first time in her life, she needed to invest in a vacuum cleaner. Course, it didn't replace her corn broom completely, because she still had plenty of other rooms to sweep.

For many years, Mom put up with 24 feet tracking dirt into the house. It wasn't a wonder that she seemed frustrated when my siblings and I came home from working out in the field and the floors were still wet from scrubbing. We haven't forgotten how she consistently exclaimed, "You barely get done, and here they come!"

Most certainly she was fighting a losing battle, and she knew it. She got some help from her daughters in the cleaning department, but she was the one who swept (by far) the most floors with a corn broom.

I can still hear the sounds of the bristles going swish... swish as she energetically swept the front cement steps. It was music to my ears.

37

11
Born in a Barn

In the colder months of the year, Mom continuously had to remind my siblings and me to shut the door between the kitchen and our unheated porch. If one of us kids neglected to close the door behind them, it didn't take her long to detect that cold air was filtering into the warm kitchen. She'd abruptly stop what she was doing and shut it for the guilty party. As she did so, she generally asked, "Were you born in a barn?"

My siblings and I knew what she meant; our barn was definitely drafty. Some of the shingles were missing on the roof, and the windows were nothing more than wide open spaces, which allowed the wind to freely blow through. On frigid, windy mornings, this atmosphere made for rather unpleasant milking conditions. Even if only a few drops of warm milk trickled down my pinkies as I hand milked a cow, the wetness quickly caused them to turn pinkish-red. In no time at all, they felt like frozen icicles.

By the time the chores were finished, I was anxious to get inside the warm house. I turned the door knob with my aching hand and rushed through the kitchen where Mom was preparing breakfast. Without saying a word, I hurried into the bathroom and began running lukewarm water over my throbbing hands. It made my fingers sting worse; but from past experience, I knew it would soon soothe them. Even over the sound of running water, I heard the door slam and Mom exclaim, "Were you born in a barn!" I immediately remembered that I hadn't shut the door.

While our barn could never take credit for being my brothers, sisters or my birthplace, it was the farm building that our mother cats sometimes sought refuge in when their time was near. Spring was the most prominent season of the year when our "fat" cats disappeared from the farmyard scene. When Judy noticed one of them was missing, she told the rest of us. Since we had several outbuildings for them to hide away in while giving birth, finding a new litter was always a challenge for us kids.

After searching in the garage and boxcar to no avail, Patty suggested, "Let's look for them in the hayloft." We climbed up the two wood ladders that led to the second level of our barn. A big pile of hay was stored up there, and we were thrilled upon hearing faint meows. We knew their nest had to be somewhere in the stack of hay, and we quickly found the cute kittens. Why, they didn't even have their eyes open, yet! More than likely, they had been born very recently. We felt like good detectives, because that mother cat didn't outsmart us for long!

Mary gently picked up a coal black kitty. There was also one with smoky gray fur and several of them had stripes. The multi-striped ones were our least favorite color. Since we outnumbered the kittens, we had to take turns holding them.

When we got tired of playing with the soft, cuddly new-borns, we went to the house and excitedly told Mom about our discovery. We listened intently as she informed us that the mother didn't appreciate us touching her babies, and she'd probably move them.

"How does she do that?" Mary asked.

"She carries one kitten at a time by the back of its neck to a new location," Mom replied. "She has to make quite a few trips to get them all moved."

The next day when we returned to the loft to play with them, the tiny kittens were gone. We were disappointed that the nest had been vacated, but we now had a new mission. We set out to discover where the litter had been moved to. As we hurriedly left the barn, we didn't have to worry about closing the big door, because it was typically left open most of the time. We were well aware of the fact that once we found the cute kitties, we could only play with them outdoors. Mom didn't let us bring animals into the house unless there was a special reason.

I recall one winter evening when Dad brought a newborn calf into the house, because it was in danger of freezing. He laid it on an old blanket in front of our propane stove. Mom had grown up on a dairy farm, so she didn't object to the dirty calf being there. When it got dry and warm, Dad carried the now frisky calf out to the barn. He had penned the mother cow up in there, and she no doubt would be thrilled to be reunited with her offspring.

Mom was also lenient about letting a new puppy stay indoors until it got used to us and its unfamiliar surroundings. While we always had a dog protecting our place, none of them ever had pups. So when we were in need of a new puppy, Dad asked around to see who had one to give away.

My siblings and I were excited when he brought a wiggly, furry one home. The newest addition to our family instantly became the center of our attention. Jackie got to hold it first, but there were a lot of eager volunteers wanting to cuddle it, too. If puppies can be spoiled, we were going to give it our best effort.

When it was bedtime, Mom told us to make a soft bed, put it in the corner of our porch and shut the door, so our new pet couldn't come into the rest of the house. It was difficult to fall asleep with loud whimpering, filtering into the bedrooms. Obviously, the puppy missed its mother and was lonely, scared or both. It was tempting to go hold it.

After several nights, the crying began to lessen considerably. When that happened, Mom put her foot down and said our puppy had to get used to staying outside, because that is where it was going to live full time. My brothers, sisters and I worried that it might run away in the dark, but it was eagerly waiting for us when we came outdoors to play with it the next morning.

While a few of the animals around our farm were born in our drafty, old barn, most of them weren't. However, Mom wondered quite often if my siblings and I were born there based upon our actions.

12
Half Stick of Gum

When money is short, there are always opportunities to cut corners, thus extending the budget. Every one of Mom's ten kids grew up knowing she was a gum stretcher. She always purchased it in large packages, and it was usually the Doublemint variety. She claimed the flavor was strong enough that you only had to chew half a stick, and she was right.

One of the times we were treated to gum was when we went to visit my aunt, uncle and cousins, who lived near Ovid, Colorado. These hour-long trips were generally taken on leisurely Sunday afternoons. Since Dad liked to check out how well other farmers' crops were growing, we often drove the back roads. In other words, we took the long way there. We had to keep our mouths busy chewing on something to avoid getting bored.

As we traveled, Mom reached inside her purse and pulled out a light-green package. The smell of mint filled the air.

She didn't have to ask the question, "Who wants gum?" She knew the answer would be unanimous amongst her children. They'd all want a whole stick, but they weren't going to get that much. She routinely tore each stick, which was wrapped in silver paper, into two pieces.

Mom handed the first piece to Joann, her youngest daughter. She then continued to dole out half sticks of gum to every outstretched hand. The scene probably resembled a mama bird feeding a nest filled with hungry babies. No one even thought about trying to get two half sticks. There were too many brothers and sisters around to tattle on them. However, if a vote had been taken in the car, my siblings and I would have agreed that the portion of gum we were chewing on seemed kind of skimpy. Still, when we arrived at our destination, we all had fresh breath.

I remember when Dad told Delores, Tom and me that we could make gum from wheat. At first, we thought he was pulling our leg. It didn't sound possible, but he insisted it was achievable. He picked up a small handful and put the golden-brown kernels into his mouth. We followed his lead. As we crunched away, our teeth slowly broke down the hard berries. A nutty sort of flavor filled our mouths. It certainly didn't taste anything like the store bought gum Mom gave us.

At first, it didn't seem like the wheat would turn into anything that resembled gum; but as we continued to chew, a little wad began to form. The earthy substance wasn't as elastic as the kind sold in stores. The hardest part was to keep the homemade version from breaking up and swallowing it. The best thing about the experience was it felt like Dad had shared a secret with us. It was something he'd learned how to do during his childhood, and now he had passed the tip along to us.

I also recall when we each got our first "full" piece of bubble gum. We just knew anything that came in such a colorful yellow, blue, red, white and pink wrapper had to be good. Inside was a bright pink cylinder of gum with a comic strip wrapped around it. It was like getting two treats in one package.

The first few chews were tough on the jaw; but before long, it became juicy and flavorful. None of us knew how to blow bubbles, but we were determined to learn together. It took quite a bit of practice before our tiny, round balls of air started growing in size. Soon, we were having a contest to see who could blow the biggest bubble. Course, the end result usually meant that when it burst, sticky pieces of gum got on our faces.

We quickly learned that bubble gum rapidly loses its elasticity and delicious flavor. The longer we chewed, the tougher it became. That wasn't true of the half stick of gum Mom rationed out to us. The Doublemint taste lasted the entire length of time we chewed it.

Perhaps, we shouldn't have ever complained about only getting half a stick of gum. More than likely, it meant we got a new piece twice as often.

13
Stacking Hay

My father was kept busy stacking hay three times a summer. The first cutting would be in June, the second one around the Fourth of July and the third in August. If the growing season lasted long enough to harvest the alfalfa a fourth time, it was almost like getting a bonus.

Harvesting our hay was done in three steps – mowing, raking and stacking. It was definitely time to cut the crop when it started blooming into a lovely mixture of deep purple, lavender and white flowers. When that happened, a wonderful sweet-smelling aroma filled the countryside. It was a shame that the picturesque scene was about to change, but Dad wasn't growing the hay for its beauty. He pulled a mower behind his tractor and began cutting the field in seven-foot strips. It usually took him all morning to mow a 20-acre field.

Whenever the mower's sickle became dull, Dad removed it for sharpening. Since it was too long for him to handle by himself, he asked his son Luke to hold the one end of the bar to keep it from bowing. For safety reasons, the grinder was mounted on an old table outdoors. As the sides of the triangular-shaped blades were being sharpened, sparks randomly flew away from the abrasive grinding wheel and a loud chattering noise could be heard throughout the farmyard.

As soon as the mowed hay was dry enough to rake, Mom changed out of her housedress and into the pair of jeans that she only wore while working in the field. She wrapped her brunette hair up in a scarf and knotted it at the front of her head. She could expertly handle our John Deere 530 tractor and rake the hay into windrows that were spaced about three feet apart. After another period of drying, she raked it again. This time, flipping the hay over and combining two windrows to make one.

When the crop was lying on the ground, Dad didn't want any rain, because the hay would mold. During the curing process, he checked it often. He wanted the hay as dry as possible but enough remaining moisture in it to keep the nutritious leaves from falling off the stems. Once it had dried to that stage, he was anxious to get it stacked.

Dad's Farmhand was mounted on his John Deere 70. As he followed a windrow, green hay was collected in the hay basket. When it was full, he drove over to a slightly raised area in the field where there was good drainage and dumped it there. As the stack grew in size, he piled it so the sides and ends were straight and the top was rounded off. It took skill to build a waterproof haystack, but he had years of experience doing so.

When Dad was out in the hot field stacking hay, he wouldn't take time out to run home for a drink and a snack. He knew one of his children would be bringing some refreshments out to him. Judy loved to get the catering assignment. "Dad's probably hungry and thirsty by now," Mom said. "Why don't you take something out to him?"

After making a sandwich and getting a cold pop out of the refrigerator, Judy hopped on her bike and rode down a dirt road. At the edge of the hayfield where Dad was working, she saw part of a chicken's wing. It still had white feathers on it. She knew a coyote had likely slipped into their yard unannounced, grabbed a plump chicken and ran off with the protesting bird in its mouth.

When Dad saw his fourth oldest daughter approaching, he brought his tractor to a stop and climbed down. "It's a hot one today," he observed, taking off his straw hat and wiping the sweat from his forehead. She handed him the snack, hoping he would like it.

Dad gladly gulped down big bites of the sandwich and guzzled the pop. "That hit the spot!" he exclaimed, handing the can back to her. Judy smiled at him, knowing he'd probably saved the last few swallows for her, because that's just the kind of father he was. "If I'm going to get this field stacked today, I best get back to work," he declared matter-of-factly.

The first cutting of alfalfa was coarser than the other ones. To keep them separate, Dad started new haystacks during the second cutting. By the end of the growing season, each of his alfalfa fields had several stacks in them, and they had become brown in color.

After all of our crops had been harvested in the fall, Dad liked to give our cattle free range. They loved having the freedom to roam into any of the fields that were within the boundaries of our small farm. There were plenty of dried sugar beet tops for them to eat. Plus, they could feast on any corn missed by the picker. It was a cheap way to keep them fed. They could also venture into the hayfields; but before he let them out, the stacks needed to be fenced in.

He didn't want the herd devouring the stored hay. Most of it was going to be sold to the grinders, and the remainder would be fed to the herd during the winter months.

On Saturday morning, Dad, my siblings and I gathered around our fence post pile, which was neatly stacked and about six-feet high. Everyone was wearing gloves to avoid getting splinters. We tossed the used wooden posts aboard our truck box. After the rest of the fencing supplies were rounded up, we drove out to an alfalfa field.

While Dad dug holes into the earth with his shovel, my siblings and I counted the number of needed posts and threw them off the truck. We then jumped down to the ground, put the posts into the holes and packed dirt around them. Tom helped Dad to tightly secure the strands of barbed wire. Before long, we were off to the next haystack to fence it in. When they were all enclosed, the cattle were turned out so they could roam and eat to their hearts content.

The hay grinders usually arrived in late fall or early winter. They brought their equipment and worked directly beside the stack. We typically had around 200 tons to sell to them. They ground the brittle stems into a powder and hauled it away in semis. It took the crew around two weeks to finish grinding our hay.

Dad always kept 15 to 20 tons of the third cutting for feed, because it was finer and better quality. He hauled it home on his hayrack and made small stacks beside the west and east sides of the corral. During the cold winter months, the herd was penned up in the corral, and he fed the hungry cattle every morning and evening. He used a pitch fork and tossed the musty-smelling hay down beside the fence. They reached through the opening and contentedly chewed until the last bite of it was gone.

Eventually, the way we harvested alfalfa around our farm was changed. Dad bought a swather, and it replaced the mowing and raking steps. Luke really enjoyed operating the new piece of machinery, because the cut hay smelled so good. However, Dad still had to stack tons of hay each summer with his Farmhand until he retired in 1982.

The days of seeing haystacks, which looked like extremely large loaves of bread out in the field, are long gone. The crop is now stored in bales, a sign of farming progress.

14
Privilege of Hunting

Each November, the pheasant's instinct to survive is tested by hunters. The game bird is crafty, liking to run ahead of its stalkers, crossover and double back behind them. Sometimes a hidden bird chooses to sit tight, and then fly away after the danger has passed on by. If it is flushed out, the long-tailed pheasant cackles loudly as it picks up altitude and speed.

Decades ago, pheasant season opened at noon. I remember eager hunters began arriving at our farm around mid-morning. Since they pulled into our yard and parked in an open area near the pigpen, it was easy to tell they weren't there to visit us. "More hunters," Dad grumbled. "I'm going to find out who it is."

He put on his hat and coat and stepped outside to talk with them. The rest of us curiously peered out of the windows. From our vantage point, it appeared that Dad was enjoying conversing with them. I do recall him coming back indoors and telling Mom that some of the hunters were from Denver and were distant relatives of ours.

Dad didn't post our land with "no trespassing signs." Many of the same hunters returned to our property on a yearly basis. Regardless if they were a new hunter or one that had been there before, he always told them that it was imperative to shut any gates they opened. Our herd of cattle was roaming about the farm, cleaning up any feed left behind from harvest. He certainly didn't want them straying onto a highway. We knew where the homemade, barbed-wire gates had been strategically placed, but the hunters or any other visitors to our place may not remember or know where they were located. Therefore, we securely tied small pieces of white rags onto the three strands of barbed wire to catch their attention. The ends of the rags freely blew in the wind.

It almost seems like yesterday when our family came home from town, turned onto our road and a gate with simple, white rags blocked our progress. "Delores, can you open and close the gate?" Dad asked.

His oldest daughter, who was sitting beside the door, got out of the warm car. She unhooked the top barbed-wire loop that was tightly fastened around a fence post. She was then able to easily remove the gate's post out of the bottom barbed-wire loop before laying the gate flat on the ground. Dad proceeded to drive over it. Once we were through, Delores closed it and hopped back inside the car. Even for us, our gates were an inconvenience. So we wondered what the hunters thought of opening and shutting them.

Just before twelve o'clock, the hunters drove their vehicles out of our yard and into our fields.Mom never cared for opening day. She worried that a stray BB might travel a distance and hit one of her children, playing in the yard. Dad didn't express concern that a cow might be accidentally shot, but he probably thought about that possibility. The sound of firing guns in the distance could be heard off and on all afternoon, making us wonder if they were getting any pheasants.

It was nothing to brag about, but we had plenty of weeds for the birds to nest in and hide among. We always raised corn; consequently, the pheasants had plenty to eat, making our land good hunting ground. Once in a while, a group of men filled their limit or went over it. On their way home, they stopped and gave us one. The kind gesture was their way of thanking us for the privilege of hunting.

Mom made cleaning a pheasant look easy. She tugged on the iridescent feathers and the skin pulled away from the meat. Its craw contained evidence that corn was a big part of its diet. The game bird was tiny compared to the chickens we raised and butchered every summer. She fried the pheasant, and it definitely had a wild taste. It was drier than chicken, but it was a nice treat for a change. We had to be careful as we ate it, though, because there was the possibility of BBs being embedded in the meat.

Eventually, the opening of pheasant season shifted from noon to sunrise. If a hunter was now serious about getting some ringnecks, it sure helped to be an early bird and crawl out of bed while it was still dark outside.

Ironically, hunters traveled for miles just to be able to hunt on our farmland. It was something Dad could have done a lot more if he chose to. On occasion, he would grab his 410 shotgun, go for a walk and bring home a game bird. However, it wasn't a pastime he was particularly interested in doing.

When Tom, Luke and Dan got old enough to handle a gun, there was a variety of wildlife around for them to hunt. We had an abundance of long-eared, long-legged jackrabbits on our property. They were definitely fast, because they could run up to 45 miles per hour. Between my three brothers, they got plenty of jackrabbits for our hungry dog.

Even though all of my brothers enjoyed hunting, Luke was the one who took to it like a duck takes to water. One of his favorite places to hunt for ducks was the neighbor's stream. He walked many miles tracking down those birds as well as other elusive wildlife.

Years ago, when the prairie was being settled, hunting was a necessity to feed ones family. Today, it is a privilege and should be appreciated as such.

15
Shopping Downtown with Parking Meters

As farm kids, it was a big adventure for us to accompany Mom to town on her shopping day. In the early 60s, gray parking meters lined the sidewalks of downtown Sterling, Colorado. They looked like soldiers standing at attention. It was as if they were waiting patiently for coins to be dropped into their slots. For each penny inserted, 12 minutes of parking time would pop up. The maximum meter time allotted was one hour, which cost the shopper a nickel. The money went to the city's revenue. At that time, the majority of stores located downtown were small, family-owned businesses. The Fair Shopping Center was still a future concept for the community.

On Saturday afternoons, downtown was always busy. It seemed like everyone in the county was shopping, making it hard to find a parking spot. I can still picture Mom driving around the block several times looking for a parking place close to the store she wanted to go into. Just as important, her eagle eyes were searching for a meter with some time still showing. When she caught sight of one, she made a beeline for it.

Mom carried a supply of pennies in her purse just for the purpose of feeding those money-eating meters. She chose a couple of her children to go to the store with her, and the others would get their turns later. But before she left, she handed several pennies to those remaining in the car with strict instructions, "Watch out for the meter maid! If you see her coming and the time has expired, put a penny in!" After getting out of the car, our mother fed the hungry meter according to the amount of time she expected to be gone. She certainly didn't want to put in any extra money.

Everyone knew what the meter maid looked like. She wore a uniform and carried a long, black stick that had a piece of chalk on the end of it. As she walked by the parked cars, she quickly put a white mark on every vehicle's front tire. An hour later, she patrolled by again. If the mark was in the same place, she wrote out a ticket, because the maximum length of time to be parked in one spot had been exceeded. She put the fine inside a small brown envelope and tucked it under the windshield wiper. She also handed out tickets to vehicles parked where the meter had expired.

Mom relied upon her "meter sitters." Whenever we saw the uniformed lady working her way down the sidewalk, we checked our meter. If it had expired, there was a flurry of activity in the car. This time it was Judy's turn to grab a penny. She swung the door open, inserted the copper-colored coin into the slot, turned the knob and hurried back inside the safety of our vehicle.

On occasion, our guard duty broke down, because we were too busy people watching. We felt like little spies, knowing they didn't realize curious eyes were observing them. Passersby seemed to be either in a big hurry or like they had all the time in the world. Another reason we might not notice the approaching meter maid was we were preoccupied with fighting. When she slipped it under the wiper, we looked at each other as if to say, "We're in trouble now." We had probably cost Mom about $1.50 in fines. She had told us before that the cost increases slightly the more tickets she got.

My favorite parking spot was right in front of JCPenney. If we got lucky, an employee would be setting up a different window display at the front of the store. As she changed the mannequin's clothing and shoes, it reminded me of my elementary school teacher redecorating the bulletin board in her classroom. The employee looked like she was doing a very important job, for lots of shoppers checked out the store's showcase.

Other times, Mom found a parking spot near the barber pole. I thought the spinning motion of the red, white and blue stripes was very pretty. The pole was prominently located on the sidewalk right in the front of the hair-cutting business. It was their way of advertising the service they offered.

If Mom decided to park near the courthouse square, the mouth-watering aroma of popcorn filled the air. Clarence's Corner was located in a tiny, canary yellow stand. Even though Clarence was handicapped, he was a successful businessman. We knew firsthand that he made the best tasting popcorn. In addition, he sold sno cones, candy and pop.

One of the stores us kids enjoyed going into was Woolworths. Just inside the front entrance doors, there was a gate-like device. Customers went through it by pushing on the top silver bar, which spun the other shorter bars in a circular motion, allowing entrance. It reminded me of busting through the line as we played red rover in grade school.

Woolworths definitely carried a unique assortment of candy. I especially liked the tiny wax bottles that were filled with colorful, flavored syrup. It was fun to bite off the top, suck out the liquid and chew the wax for gum.

Near the candy display was the pet department. It was entertaining to watch the graceful fish swimming around in tanks. Course, the vivid, talkative parakeets certainly got their fair share of attention, as well. Even though we had plenty of birds singing in our trees on the farm, none of them were as vibrant or as smart as those caged birds at Woolworths.

The five-and-dime store carried plenty of variety. They sold towels, bedspreads, stationery, yarn, puzzles, toys, etc. When we were in the store around noon, there were customers sitting on stools at the luncheon counter. The menu featured sandwiches and items from their old-fashioned soda fountain. My eyes were invariably drawn to the three large, plastic beverage containers, sitting on the counter. They held colorful red, yellow and green drinks. As the liquids circulated, they sounded like gurgling, miniature waterfalls. Mom never bought us kids any, so we had no idea if the drinks tasted as good as they looked. We could only imagine.

Those who accompanied Mom into Woolworths knew she would never linger there long. She'd buy what she needed and hurry back to the car where her other restless kids were waiting. Hopefully, her "meter sitters" had done their job successfully.

16
Figured by Hand

The business end of farming has changed immensely over the years. While most farmers now rely upon computers to keep accurate records of their operation, I remember the time when Dad never even owned a calculator.

On snowy winter days in the 1960s, Dad was often found sitting at the kitchen table, working on his income taxes. He separated out crumpled sales tickets for gas, seed, repair parts, plus all sorts of other expenses the farm had incurred during the year. In another pile, he placed paperwork for the farm's income. There were check stubs for the sale of livestock and the crops we had sold.

When he wanted some assistance, he called his four older children over. Delores, Tom, Patty and I took our seats at the kitchen table. He handed each of us a pencil and a piece of scratch paper. "I need your help in adding up some numbers. Write them down in dollar and cents figures as

I give them to you," he instructed. He then read a series of numbers that went something like this, "$72.68, 92.84, 86.59, 102.50, 5.63, 19.24, 18.23 and 41.60. Add those."

My siblings and I drew a line under the list of numbers. We hurriedly added them, hoping to be the first one finished; and, of course, come up with the right answer. Since Patty was the youngest one helping, we waited for her to finish before telling Dad what amount we came up with. When the majority of us got the same total, he jotted that amount down on his paper. If everyone came up with a different answer, we redid the problem. We spent hours adding and subtracting sets of numbers that Dad gave us.

Us kids didn't know what all the money figures meant, but we felt important helping Dad with his income taxes. It was also a way for us to improve our math skills. It was almost as much fun as participating in arithmetic races at school. The teacher chose several students to go up to the green chalkboard, while the remainder of the class stayed in their seats. We jotted down the numbers she gave us with a piece of chalk and tallied up the total as quickly as possible. We eagerly listened to the teacher tell us which student had come up with the correct answer first. It was then time to pick up an eraser and wipe the chalkboard clean, making it ready for the next group. While we were learning, it felt more like a game.

Dad was appreciative of the fact that we had studied hard in school, so we could help him do the preliminary preparation work for his income taxes. Once that was finished, he bundled up his information and went to town where he had a professional finish preparing his federal and state income tax returns.

I recall one particular snowy afternoon when Dad came home from the accountant's office in a rather bad mood. He told Mom, "My vehicle was the only one parked on the whole block. I didn't see any point in putting money into the parking meter. I assumed the weather was so bad that the meter maid wasn't even walking around the streets checking meters. When I came back to the pickup, there was a ticket under the windshield wiper! Why would you give someone a ticket when the rest of the block was available for parking?"

"The city must need the money more than we do!" Mom exclaimed. But like good citizens, my parents paid the fine and forgot about the ordeal.

Throughout the following year, Dad placed all of his tax-related paperwork in the proper pockets in his brown expanding file folder. As the months passed by, the folder filled up to capacity, and the papers became increasingly wrinkled. In that condition, they didn't look like they had any value, but they did contain the information he'd need to report another busy growing season's activity.

Dad didn't see any reason to buy a calculator. Sure it might have been faster, but the answers would have been the same. So whenever he was ready to organize his income tax information, he always called upon willing kids to assist him. Once they were seated at the kitchen table, he handed each of them a piece of scratch paper and fittingly a pencil that had obviously been hand sharpened with a knife.

Since then, many tax seasons have come and gone. But I can still hear Dad's voice as he gave us a list of dollar figures before saying, "Add those." Simply put, it also added up to become a wonderful childhood memory.

17
Tin
Lunch Box

During my grade school years, I didn't want to eat school lunches, because I was used to Mom's cooking and that's the way I wanted to keep it. She did her best to convince me that eating a hot meal would taste better than a cold one. However, I stubbornly refused. I continued carrying my light brown tin lunch box by its red plastic handle to the small country school in Padroni.

There usually wasn't any surprise waiting for me when I opened it at noon. It generally contained a peanut butter and jelly sandwich, potato chips and an apple. Mom suggested that I buy a carton of milk to go with my meal. It would have only cost three cents; but I didn't care for the dairy product, so I ate my food without drinking anything with it. When I was finished eating, I put the empty plastic bags and any scraps back into my lunch box, closed the lid and flipped up the latch. I took the much lighter container back to my classroom and hurried outdoors to play. At the end of the school day, I consistently carried it and my books onto the bus with me.

After supper, my tin lunch box was washed and dried along with the other dishes. It was white on the inside but was showing signs of rust, because it had been washed repeatedly. Mom then packed my lunch for the next school day. I think she got just as tired of the routine as I did of eating the same basic foods.

In sixth grade, I finally decided to get brave. I went through the line like the rest of the students, and it seemed foreign to carry a tray to the table. To my surprise, the meal tasted much better than I'd expected. In the process, I discovered some new foods. Mom never fixed navy beans and ham. The first time it was on the menu, I thought it was very flavorful. My favorite main dish soon became chicken and noodles, which had a creamy sauce. Our head cook either had a secret recipe, or else she just happened to hit my taste buds exactly right.

On the last day of school, we were traditionally dismissed in the early afternoon, and the cooks didn't have to prepare lunch. Instead the mothers brought a covered dish, and they joined the students and teachers at a potluck. Mom never came, because she had to care for my younger brothers and sisters who weren't school age.

For dessert, the school furnished vanilla ice cream that was packaged in wax cups. The single-serving size had a lid with a tiny tab on it. To open the container, all we had to do was lift up on the flap. Each person also received a mini wooden spoon that was wrapped in paper. It didn't look like a typical spoon, because it was flat and about three inches long. Both ends were rounded off, and the center of it was a smaller diameter. The disposable eating utensil was cute, but on the downside it gave the creamy, cold treat a distinct wood flavor.

When the bell rang, it was time to head back to the classroom and gather up our used school supplies, jacket and whatever else we had there. The buses were parked out front, waiting for the excited students to load.

I recall one spring when Delores, Tom, Patty and I got a wild notion that we wanted to walk home from school on the last day. Our farm was about five miles southeast of the blonde brick building. A few days before school was to be dismissed for the summer, my siblings and I tried to persuade Mom that we could easily walk the distance and arrive home safely. It sounded like great fun, and we were convinced that the adventure would make the last day extra special.

However, Mom firmly stood her ground and said, "No!" More than likely, she made the right decision. While we knew the route by heart, my brother, sisters and I probably would have cut across the countryside to explore unfamiliar surroundings rather than follow the highway. By the time we got home, Mom would have had plenty of time to worry.

Like usual, we rode the yellow bus, and the driver dropped us off at our road. We walked the half-mile home, which was nothing new for us. Even though we weren't able to fulfill our adventure by walking all the way home, we were overjoyed that school was out for several months. We were free!

But Mom was probably thinking, "It's going to be a long summer!"

Dad, on the other hand, was likely thinking, "Good. Now we'll get a lot more sugar beets thinned since they can be out in the field all day instead of just after school."

Us kids couldn't win for losing.

18
Creamery and Homemade Ice Cream

My parents, like many other farmers in the Sterling area, sold cream to the local creamery. To me the business was intriguing, because it wasn't anything like the downtown stores. It definitely had a country atmosphere rather than a city feel.

What I remember the most about the creamery was its distinct, mildly rancid smell. Since the empty cream cans had been washed out with scalding water, it was usually steamy in the building. They were hung upside down on a rack to dry. Once in a while, the cement floor was wet, because it had been recently hosed down.

Mom and Dad owned two five-gallon cream cans. Every morning and evening, we separated the cream from the milk with an electric separator. Each milking would only fill a portion of a cream can. We continued using the same metal container until it was full, and then we switched to the other one. In the colder months of the year, the cans sat out in our unheated porch beside the separator, and we took the saved dairy product into town once a week. During the summer, the heavy cans were lugged down to our cool cellar, and the cream was hauled into town twice a week to keep it from getting overly sour.

After we dropped our full cans off at the creamery, we did other errands around town. In the meantime, the owner weighed our sour cream and tested it for butterfat content. He poured it into a large container in the cooler. Our cans were washed and ready for pick up in about an hour.

By the time we returned, a check had already been written. Mom remembers that it was usually between 25 and 30 dollars. She told me that the owner never complained that our cream was too sour, but a higher price was paid for sweet cream. Like other farm families who sold their cream to the business, my parents spent the money at the grocery store. It was always out last stop of the day.

Mom also sold her extra eggs to the creamery. She had an old, wooden crate that came with dimpled, cardboard inserts. The eggs fit nicely into the depressions, and the partitions could be stacked upon each other. The eggs were candled, and we were paid according to grade.

The owner told my parents that the eggs and cream he collected each day were loaded on a truck in the evening and sent to Denver. He sold it to various big city dairies. They used the farm-raised products to make cheese, butter, ice cream, etc., and marketed their processed goods to grocery stores and other retail facilities. Thus, the local creamery really was the middle-man operation between area farmers and big city dairies. My parents were grateful that the unique business was conveniently located only 15 miles from our farm.

However, we didn't sell all of our thick, rich cream to the local establishment. Whenever Mom wanted some for our own use, she caught a jar of it while we were doing the separating. During the summer months, she made homemade vanilla ice cream with it. She used a recipe, which called for fresh sweet cream and eggs.

After mixing up the ingredients, Mom set up a workstation on the front cement step, and it became the kids' job to turn the handle of our ice cream maker. At first, it was easy. The silver metal container virtually spun round and round in the wood bucket with minimal effort. The crunching sound of ice and rock salt overpowered the quietness of the outdoors.

At the moment, Mary was turning the handle. Once she decided that she had done her fair share, Joann took over the duty until she got tired. The task was then passed on to another sibling. Every once in awhile, we added more salt just to make sure the ice stayed really cold. We certainly didn't want to churn any longer than we had to!

It took a long time for the mixture to thicken. When that started to happen, it got harder and harder to crank at a steady pace. We were always happy when Mom checked it and said our job was finished. She removed the silver metal bucket, took it into the kitchen and scraped off the paddle. She replaced the lid on the container and put it in the deep freezer where it would remain until we had eaten our Sunday dinner.

Homemade ice cream quickly disappeared around our household. It was more granular than the ice cream Mom bought at the grocery store, but it had a delicious, made from scratch taste. While it took plenty of extra effort to whip up a batch, we thought it was worth it.

On the other hand, us kids weren't as crazy about the whole milk Mom saved for our family's use. She poured the warm liquid directly from a milk bucket, through a cloth to strain it and into the pitcher. After it got cold in the refrigerator, a layer of cream would rise to the surface. My siblings and I always skimmed the thick, yellowish coating off the best we could, because we didn't like it floating around in our cereal.

Through the years, the girls in the family all learned firsthand how long it took to clean the electric separator, which had a slightly sour smell. It was quite a task to wash the many dirty parts, and this time Patty got stuck with that duty while Judy dried. There was a whole stack of cone-shaped disks that fit over a shaft. It seemed to take forever to wash and dry the thin, silver disks individually.

Us girls didn't fully understand how the many parts of the electric separator worked together to dispense milk and cream through two different spouts. More importantly, we knew how to reassemble the intriguing components, so our separator would be ready to do its job right after the next milking was finished.

19
Around the Schoolyard

The grade school that my siblings and I attended was located at the edge of the tiny town of Padroni. On the north side of the school's property, there was a barbed-wire fence, separating the playground from a pasture. A couple of pretty, brown horses lived there, who spent most of their time grazing on the long grass. They probably knew when the students were having recess, for the quietness of the countryside was erased.

Sometimes during recess, my friend Ila and I played house under the cottonwood trees near the pasture. We used our hands to scoop dirt together and create rooms for our make-believe homes. On one particular morning, we stopped playing when we heard the horses whinny. They had come up to the fence and were looking our direction. We got up off the ground, ran over to them and petted their foreheads. The teachers didn't care if we gave them a little attention.

During other recesses, I played softball, football or dodge-ball. The only playground equipment we had to choose from was a swing, merry-go-round, slide, tetherball and a teeter-totter. I really enjoyed the teeter-totter. The heavy metal framework supported two seesaws that were painted a bright red. The wide, wooden planks didn't have any handles to hold onto. In order to keep from falling off, the students had to grasp their hands around the thick board.

Even at a young age, it soon became apparent to me just how important it was to find someone who weighed about the same amount. If the weight difference was too great, adjustments could be made to balance it out by one person scooting closer to the pivot point. Another option was to find a third student to teeter-totter with us. Then, the two lightest kids were paired up on one side, and the heavier one went solo on the other end. The real challenge came when we tried to balance the plank. It was hard to keep it level and steady; but with perseverance, it could be accomplished.

While it was fun to seesaw, it was exercise, too. We had to use our legs to push with so we'd pivot up and down. Inevitably, it was only a matter of time until one of us would suspend the other person in midair. Whenever my legs were helplessly dangling, I watched carefully for a quick shove of the other person's feet. I knew that meant the tee-ter-totter would be going down rapidly.

As I got older, tetherball became my favorite recess pastime. In this game, height instead of weight was an important factor. My sister Delores was less than two years older than me. She was taller but not a whole lot; thus, we made good opponents. Plus, we both had a lot of endur-ance, having done our share of work around the farm.

A yellow tetherball was attached to a rope, which was hanging from the top of the tall, silver pole. The base of it was cemented in place and deep grooves had been worn into the sandy soil from previous competitions. We stood on opposite sides of the metal pole. There was an imaginary line dividing our playing area into equal portions. We couldn't cross over it without getting into the opponent's space.

"You can serve first," Delores offered.

Trying to catch her off guard, I quickly smacked the ball with my right fist. It swung over her head several times before she hit it hard with the palms of her hands, causing the rope to nearly unwind all the way. We battled back and forth, jumping when necessary to return the ball the opposite way. When Delores finally wrapped the rope completely around the pole, she won the game.

The tetherball pole wasn't the tallest one in our schoolyard. Our flagpole looked very stately, because it had an official purpose. When I entered the sixth grade, the teacher told our class that it was going to be our duty to put the flag up at the beginning of school and take it down at the end of the day. In order to demonstrate, she took us outdoors where we gathered around her. She showed us how to put the hooks in the proper holes, raise the flag up the silver pole and bring it back down. She demonstrated several times the proper method to fold the rectangular material. She stressed that the cloth should never touch the ground. If it did, the flag would need to be burned and a new one purchased.

Back in the classroom, she divided us into pairs and made up a schedule. Each team had flag duty for one week before the next couple of students took over. My partner was Sue, and we took our responsibility seriously. We were very careful not to let the stars or stripes touch the ground. The hardest part of our assignment was folding the heavy cloth neatly at the end of the day. After we became more comfortable with taking care of our country's symbol, we began to relax.

All went smoothly until one morning when the teacher informed the whole class, "A resident of the community drove by and noticed the flag was flying upside down. He immediately called the school." She then looked directly at Sue and me and stressed, "A flag flying upside down means our country is in distress! You need to go back outdoors and correct the mistake you made!"

As we walked outside, both of us expressed our embarrassment. We lowered the flag, turned the cloth around so that the stars were in the upper left-hand corner. Soon, Old Glory was back at the top of the pole, waving majestically in the breeze.

A valuable lesson was learned that day. The teacher and principal continued to trust the sixth-grade class to care for the national symbol. From then on, it always looked exactly like every other flag, flying freely over the land of the United States.

20
Kool-Aid Parties

M om routinely went to town on Wednesday afternoons to shop and run errands. When her oldest
daughters reached the baby-sitting age, she was
probably relieved. At least during the summer months, she
could leave most of her kids at home. She'd take a couple
of them along, basing her decision upon who hadn't gone
to town for awhile.

Since Dad was out in the field working, that gave my
siblings and me plenty of free time to use our imaginations.
We could certainly come up with a variety of ways to enter-
tain ourselves. Although we never had permission to have
Kool-Aid parties, we had our share of them. We were fairly
certain Mom wouldn't want us sitting around the kitchen
table sipping, slurping and worst of all spilling the sticky
drink. Thus, we felt guilty while having fun. The refresh-
ing drink sure tasted good on a hot day. Sometimes we ate
cookies or peanut butter and jelly sandwiches with it.

Whenever we decided to have a party, we first had to agree on what flavor of Kool-Aid to make. As I recall, lemon-lime won out more often than not. The drink was simple to make. After ripping open the package and pouring the powdery mix into a two-quart Tupperware pitcher, we added a cup of sugar, filled it with water and stirred.

Everyone gathered around the table where we laughed and talked while thoroughly enjoying our refreshments. We refilled our Tupperware cups and drank until the pitcher was empty. Nobody was eager to clean up the mess; but we were well aware of the fact that if Mom came home early, we'd be in trouble for sure. As we did the dishes, it felt like we were getting rid of the evidence.

Once the kitchen looked presentable, we agreed to play the game button, button, who's got the button. Mom had a jar filled with buttons that she had cut off of old garments. Mary selected a pretty one, and she was going to be the first person "it." The rest of us were sitting in a circle with our hands out and palms together. As she went from person to person, she placed the bottom of her hands over her siblings' hands. They in turn opened the tops of theirs slightly, so she could drop the button in if she decided to. After going completely around the group, she asked, "Button, button, who's got the button?"

Luke was the first player to take a guess. "I think Tom has it." But he was wrong.

It was then Patty's turn to guess. With the button safely tucked in her hands, she tried to confuse the others by saying, "Judy's got the button." She did her best not to smile and give herself away. The round was over when I guessed Patty. She then became the leader or "it."

After we got bored with that game, we found plenty of other ways to occupy ourselves. Course, most of our activities resulted in making the place a bigger mess. Around

4:30 p.m., it was as if an alarm sounded at our household. We knew Mom and the others would be home about five o'clock. It was time to scramble about and get everything back in order.

Patty wrote down a variety of jobs on slips of paper, put them into a small box, and we drew our assignments. It didn't take us long to finish cleaning. I'm not sure if it was because we had lots of people to help, or we didn't do a very thorough job.

The second Mom walked into the house, the answer to that question was confirmed. "What a pigpen!" she exclaimed. If she had gotten home about a half-an-hour earlier, she would have noticed that we at least made an effort to straighten things up. She didn't stay angry at us for long, though. Perhaps it was because we helped carry the groceries in and put them away. I noticed that she had bought ten packages of Kool-Aid. It was a good thing she did, for our supply was getting low.

Our family never drank pop with our dinner and supper meals, but we enjoyed our share of Kool-Aid. Back then, it was relatively cheap to make. The product was advertised on TV a lot, and it was a popular beverage choice for many American families. The round, clear pitcher with the smiling face made it look especially appealing. So when Mom asked one of us girls to make a pitcher of it, we were eager to do so. We never had to read the directions first, because we already had plenty of practice at making it to perfection.

As I recall, Mom never figured out that we made Kool-Aid when she was in town. Nor do I think anyone ever tattled, because my siblings and I really liked having those secret parties.

21
Cards, Pool and Candy

As a farmer, Dad worked very hard during the spring, summer and fall months. Winter was his slowest season of the year. It was a chance for him to kick back and spend some of his free time doing what he enjoyed.

Since we lived in an agricultural area, there were plenty of men around who were in the same shoes. In the afternoons, their favorite gathering place was a local pool hall. The business was located in the sleepy, little town of Padroni, Colorado. Depending upon how many men showed up that particular day, determined whether a friendly game of cards was being played or a competitive game of pool. If the turnout was good, then both forms of entertainment might be taking place at the same time. No doubt, the men also talked a great deal about the weather and farm-related issues.

For us kids, Dad going to the pool hall meant something entirely different. We liked it when he came home with the smell of smoke on his coat, and he pulled out a brown paper bag from his pocket. That signified he'd won candy either from playing cards or from shooting pool, and we were going to benefit from it. Typically, a whole variety of sweets were inside the bag, ranging from jawbreakers, suckers, bubble gum, Tootsie Rolls, Bit-O-Honey, etc.

Dad's youngest child always got to look in the bag first and select a treat. The next youngest in line would get second choice. By the time the sack had reached the oldest daughter, it had been passed around many times. The best candy most likely was already gone.

When Dad came home empty-handed quite a few times in a row, Mom knew that he'd been on a losing streak. Perhaps that didn't matter; for I am sure, he still had fun socializing with the other men.

The pool hall was a tall, white building with a screen door at the entrance. Very few businesses were still operating in the dying town, so it looked rather lonely. Patrons of the establishment parked on Main Street, which was a graveled road. There wasn't a paved street in the entire town. Being a girl, I wasn't allowed to go inside the big building, but I was curious. So I asked my dad, "What's the inside of the pool hall look like?"

"It's just an old, dark building with wood floors that creak when someone walks on them," he replied matter-of-factly. "It smells bad in there, because some of the men smoke cigarettes. They've got a bar, but nobody drinks anything but pop during the day anyway. It's just a good place for farmers to hang out on cold, winter days."

My youngest brother Dan occasionally got to share in that phase of his father's life. One of his first childhood memories was going to the pool hall with him. While Dad shot pool with his buddies, the shy, young boy sometimes sat under the rectangular table, or he explored the run-down building. He looked forward to the men taking a break, for Dad would buy him a pop and candy bar from his winnings.

As a teenager, my husband Ben remembers that pool halls were a good way to interact with the old men. The only thing they might have in common with each other was picking up a cue stick, taking a break shot and hitting balls into pockets. That shared interest was plenty in itself. It was a way for two generations to have a friendly competition without spending much money in the process.

When school wasn't in session because of a snow day, Ben enjoyed spending time down at the pool hall. He recalls that the older men liked seeing young guys get interested in the sport they loved. They didn't have any problem taking them under their wings and teaching them how to play snooker or eight ball. But since they were the veteran players, they typically won.

The era when pool halls were a popular recreational spot has passed on by. As the businesses were closed down one after another, it was like a series of dominoes tumbling. Perhaps it was from lack of interest, because people found new forms of entertainment. Thus, the owners couldn't make enough profit to keep the doors open. Whatever the reason, plenty of WW11 veterans (like my dad) thoroughly enjoyed the laid-back, male-oriented hangouts while they lasted.

Old-fashioned pool halls weren't just a good place for older men and a few teenagers to gather and pass some time. It was also a special setting where fathers and sons could go and bond without Moms or sisters being around.

22
Rock Collecting

M etal detectors are used by hobbyists to discover hidden treasures buried beneath the surface. The excitement rises when a signal sounds, alerting the operator to dig in that location. It could turn up something valuable or just an ordinary piece of junk.

Years ago, my brothers, sisters and I had lots of fun doing something similar only our treasures were in plain sight. We were rock collectors. How can you get more down to earth than that?

Most of our searching for rocks was done on a road that had been worn into the buffalo grass in our pasture. For decades, the route was used as a shortcut to our mailbox. In the process, "jewels of the earth" had worked their way up to the surface of the ruts.

We walked tentatively, eyes focused on the ground, eager to find our next precious discovery. Sometimes the color is what caught our eye. We especially liked smooth, shiny rocks that looked like they had been polished. If a stone had become split, the sparkly core was attractive to us. Other times, the unique shape is what drew our attention to it. Often, the whole group came to a stop to admire the latest find. The rocks that did not meet our criteria were aimlessly tossed back to the land. They could stay there for the next 100 years for all we cared. Those that were keepers were carefully slipped into our pockets.

While we were out rock collecting, we did our best to avoid the numerous cactuses that thrived there. Many of them were hard to see, because they grew close to the pasture's surface. Sometimes we wandered off the trail just to admire the lovely flowers that were blooming on the sharp, prickly plants. Our pasture was also home for lots of burrowing gophers. They had slender, brown bodies with stripes running down their backs. Rarely did we get close to them, for they were as fast as lightning. They certainly weren't tame enough to catch.

After we got tired of searching for rocks, we'd head home with our collection. More than likely, the treasures that we had accumulated would only remain valuable to us for a short while. The real fun was in the hunt and discovery.

Petrified wood, on the other hand, was a special, treasured find. Remarkably, it had retained the characteristics of a piece of wood. Somehow it had gotten preserved without rotting away. Our curiosity caused us to wonder how long it had actually taken to turn into stone.

In the early years of our rock collecting, our imaginations never sparked us to decorate rocks, which weren't beautiful on their own accord. Not even in our wildest dreams did we ever think about making a pet out of a silly, lifeless rock. If we wanted to get attached to an animal, we always had a dog, a bunch of cats and kittens, cattle, horse and even pigs to choose from. They all needed to be fed and cared for.

All that changed, though, when a new contest was introduced at the Logan County Fair. My younger sister Jackie told her mother, "I want to enter the pet rock contest." Mom agreed, and soon the young collector was out searching for a prize-winning rock.

Actually two rocks caught her eye. She thought the triangular-shaped one would make a good face and a really pointy rock was perfect for a witch's nose. She ventured out into our cornfield and gathered corn silk for the hair. She carefully followed the rules and used her crafting skills.

On a hot day in August, we took her entry to the fairgrounds in Sterling. We were among a throng of spectators, waiting for the judges' decision. They had a wide variety of charming pet rocks to choose from. It was a proud moment for Jackie when her creative effort was declared a winner.

In the mid 70s, pet rocks were sold in stores. The custom-made cardboard packaging also doubled as a pet carrier. It had breathing holes for the make-believe animal. In reality, the pet rock was just an ordinary, gray stone. A straw bed, instructions on how to care for the pet and tricks the new owner could teach it were included. The fad never lasted long; but while it was popular, not one of us kids ever got brave enough to ask Mom, "Will you buy me a pet rock?"

If we had, she surely would have responded, "Go make yourself one like your sister Jackie did. We've got lots of rocks around here for you to choose from."

23
Full-Service Gas Station

L ike a typical farm family, we had a large gas tank on the outer perimeters of our graveled yard. Thus, it was very convenient to fill up our tractors, trucks, pickup and car.

My sister Mary recalls an incident that happened when she was about seven years old. She was pretending to drive while Mom was busy filling up our station wagon. She pushed down on the clutch; and much to her surprise, the emerald green car proceeded to roll down a slope. She froze, but her mother yanked open the driver's door and told her to scoot over. Once Mary's foot came off the clutch, the car came to a sudden stop and no harm was done.

Even though our family didn't need to buy gas, we often stopped at a filling station when we were in town. My uncles bought the business in 1957 and operated it for many years until changing times forced them to close it. In the meantime, we got to experience the behind-the-scenes atmosphere of a full-service gas station.

For my brothers, sisters and me, it was a place we could walk into and feel at home. If we needed to use the restroom, there was a key hanging by the entrance door. Since we were family, we simply took it off the hook, went back outside and unlocked the door on the west side of the building. We were always careful to lock the restroom and hang the key back up where it belonged.

On many occasions, a group of men would be gathered around a table, playing cards. One of the owners would have to sit out and wait on customers. It was easy to see when a car drove in. There were two big picture windows on the north and west walls of the station. As the vehicle drove over the hose that was strung across the lot, a bell rang inside the building. It was a good backup just in case their arrival had been missed.

It didn't matter what the weather was like, the customer didn't have to get out of his or her comfortable vehicle. An attendant hurried outside to provide speedy service. After the initial greeting came the familiar question, "Fill 'er up?" The old-style pump had a rotating dial. It quickly cycled as the fuel guzzled into the tank.

Meanwhile, the customer's windshield and windows were washed. It was the station's policy not to charge extra to test tire pressures. Sometimes the hood was opened and the belts, oil and water levels were checked. After all, it was a full-service gas station. Customers paid a little more per gallon than at a self-service station, so they expected the royal treatment.

Occasionally, patrons chose to come inside to buy a snack. The cash register was sitting on a glass counter. Beneath it was an assortment of candy and gum. Since the sliding door was only on the side of the attendant, he pulled out the item(s) that the shopper wished to purchase.

Near the cash register, a display of batteries lined some shelves. Along another wall, a selection of tires was exhibited. Customers purchasing either of these new items could have them installed in the maintenance shop, which was located in the east end of the station.

The shop consisted of two bays and one hoist. The mechanic did all sorts of small maintenance jobs like changing oil, installing new belts, replacing brakes and fixing flat tires. The sound of an impact wrench often drifted into the main part of the building.

The business also sold pop, and Mom liked to purchase it by the case. The wooden box had slots for the glass bottles to sit individually in. They were marked with the words "return for deposit." Although it certainly wasn't required, our family always washed out the empty bottles before we took them back. They had been stored in our car garage where plenty of dirt, spider webs and dead bugs collected in them.

A lot of times, Dad stayed at the station to play cards with the men while the rest of us went downtown shopping. One day, upon our return, Mom went inside to get her card playing husband. Mary couldn't resist sliding over into the driver's seat. She should have remembered from a previous experience that pushing down on the clutch might have consequences, but she didn't. It frightened her when our car started to roll back into a busy street. Thankfully, her oldest sister Delores yelled, "Step on the brake!" She did, and the car came to a sudden stop. The close call most certainly got someone's attention inside the station, for a group of anxious adults came running out.

Dad opened the car door, looked directly at Mary and said sternly, "Don't you ever pull a stunt like that again!"

She got his message and sheepishly climbed into the middle seat with her siblings.

As we left the lot, Dad drove over the hose, ringing the bell inside the full-service gas station. But this time, an attendant didn't need to quickly respond.

24
More Than
a Propane Tank

Propane tanks are a common sight in farmyards. The one we owned had a large holding capacity, and the stored gas was mainly used to heat our house in the colder months. It was painted white, and the dome that housed the regulator was a faded red color. The tank's short legs sat on big blocks of wood right beside our kitchen.

My siblings and I thoroughly enjoyed our propane tank for a whole variety of reasons. In the warmer months, we liked to perch on top of it, because the metal was cool. If the kitchen window was open, we felt like little spies, peering inside and listening to the activity taking place there.

We had a rather unique way of mounting the tank. We'd stand back a distance, quickly sprint and grab hold of the loop-shaped metal handle on the end. In a swinging motion, we would straddle our legs over the back of our imaginary horse and pretend that we were riding bareback. Our tank's sturdy handle also served as a terrific jump rope turner. It almost worked as well as a human hand. We'd tie a rope around it and decide who would turn the other end in a clockwise, circular motion.

The rope was long enough that Jackie and Joann were having fun at the same time. They were facing each other, giggling and jumping in unison over the braided twine cord, which made a neat slapping sound as it hit the hard ground. When Joann's foot caught the rope, it came to a sudden stop, and she had to take over the turning duty.

Timing was critical in jumping rope. We had to make an entrance at the right point and stay in sync with how fast it was moving. If someone got tired of jumping and wanted to quit, exiting at the precise second was also important.

My sisters and I enjoyed singing rhymes as we jumped rope. One of our favorites was, "Cinderella dressed in yella, went upstairs to kiss a fella, made a mistake and kissed a snake. How many doctors did it take? One, two, three…" The counting continued until someone caused the rope to come to a ceasing halt.

The propane tank also became an important apparatus for us when we made our first pair of stilts. We got the idea from the neighbor's kids, who also happened to be our second cousins. They told us about the pair of stilts they'd constructed. They emphasized how much fun they were to walk on, so we decided to build a set, too.

First, we found a couple of old boards, and Tom began cutting the rough wood with a handsaw. He made L-shaped handles for us to hold onto. He nailed a block of wood on each board, so our feet would be about a foot from the ground. We found a couple of short pieces of leather straps in our barn. They were aged and cracked, but we thought they'd work. He nailed a piece of strap on the edge of a foot peg and on the main board, forming a loop. He then did the same to the other board. The straps would keep our feet from slipping off the footrests.

Once again, the propane tank came in mighty handy. We leaned up against it as we situated our feet in the loops. The stilts didn't make us a whole lot taller, but they definitely felt foreign to us. At first, they were very challenging. It took coordination, and the weight of the boards seemed to get heavier the further we walked around the yard. After we got brave enough, we tested our ability by going up the front steps of the house with our wooden legs. Even though there were just two steps to navigate, it was quite scary. Then, of course, we had to awkwardly turn around and maneuver our way back down to ground level. This took plenty of concentration and skill.

One summer day, we went over and visited our second cousins. We couldn't believe our eyes. Their stilts made ours look like baby ones. They even had to climb up on a small building and mount them from the edge of the roof. We were in awe! It was almost like watching circus performers. We admired their bravery, but we also thought they were crazy.

When we got home, the first thing we did was design a second pair of stilts, which were probably three times taller than the first set. Even so, they weren't nearly as difficult as those our second cousins expertly strolled about on. We now needed to lean our "legs of wood" against the propane tank and climb up on the tank to get our feet situated on the footrests. We walked cumbersomely around the yard with no thought of maneuvering the steps with this pair.

My siblings and I fell off of our challenging homemade stilts a few times; but fortunately, no one ever got hurt. For the most part, our only goal was to keep from stumbling and falling before making our way back to the tank for a dismount. It was a perfect place to sit down and allow the weighty boards to tumble to the ground. The next person wanting to walk around the yard like a circus performer knew exactly where to find them; they'd be right beside the propane tank where the last stunt walker had left them.

So it's probably safe to conclude that our propane tank truly "fueled" my brothers, sisters and my imaginations to reach new heights.

25
Huge Culvert

M y brothers, sisters and I liked to play in out-of-the-way places. One of our favorite sites was a huge culvert. It was buried under the paved highway that ran alongside the northern border of our farm. There usually was a small amount of water flowing through the round, corrugated metal structure. It dumped the clear water into a small creek that veered off into the neighbor's pasture.

On hot summer days, the huge culvert attracted my siblings and me like a magnet. Although we had to walk a half mile to reach our hideaway, it was worth it. The semidarkness of the large tunnel made it a refreshingly cool place to play.

Depending upon how much water was in the stream that particular day, it was sometimes difficult to step up into the silver, corrugated metal structure without getting our shoes wet. As the water exited the culvert, it created a miniature waterfall. So we sometimes had to climb up the embankment beside the culvert and carefully work our way over to the bottom edge of it. Then, we were able to straddle the gurgling water.

Once inside the shady tunnel, we followed the leader by jumping over the moving water in a zigzag pattern. We tried to go from one end of the passageway to the other as fast as we could, but the curved edge of the metal made it challenging. The older kids had to crouch slightly to prevent bumping their heads on the top of the culvert. Plus, there were large nuts and bolts, holding the sections of metal together. If a foot landed on them, it would hurt. As we amused ourselves, happy voices and young laughter echoed in our hollow hideout.

The paved county road didn't have a lot of traffic, but we could always tell when a vehicle traveled over the culvert. It sounded like rumbling thunder, and we loved it. The passersby had no idea we were underneath.

During the school year, this highway was also where the bus picked us up and dropped us off. If we arrived at our destination early on a warm morning, we sometimes ventured over to the nearby creek and enjoyed playing inside our secret place. To keep from missing our ride, someone stood on the edge of the road just above the culvert and acted as a lookout. When those in the tunnel were alerted that the bus was on the hill picking up the neighbor's kids, they hurried out of the creek bottom and waited for the arrival of the bus.

On one such morning, Jackie was the lookout while the rest of us kids spent the extra time inside the huge tunnel. About ten minutes later, she yelled, "The bus is coming!"

We hustled over to the highway. As my sister Mary picked up a book and her Hula Hoop that were lying on the ground, she expressed being nervous about the school's talent show. It was scheduled for that day. As a third grader, she was going to be competing against all of the other contestants from kindergarten to eighth grade.

In the afternoon, the students and faculty met in the gym to watch the performances. When it was Mary's turn, she stepped shyly out onto the stage with her bright pink Hula Hoop. She was wearing a yellow dress with white lace and purple socks. I knew she was well prepared, having practiced her routine many times in our graveled farmyard. Only now, there was an audience to analyze her every move.

When the peppy, patriotic music of "Stars and Stripes Forever" began playing, Mary swung into action. She appeared to be relieved when it was over. Thankfully, she never dropped the Hula Hoop once. It would have been so embarrassing if the circular, plastic tube had rolled off the stage and down into the audience. Mary looked thrilled when her name was announced as the third-place winner. For her efforts, she received a trophy.

Shortly after the talent show ended, school was dismissed for the day. Like usual, we boarded the bus for the ride home. Just before the driver dropped us kids off at our road, he drove over the huge culvert. It had been a long day at school, and nobody was interested in playing in our secret hideaway now. But it would only be a matter of time before my brothers, sisters and I ventured into the hollow tunnel to fill it with noise and laughter.

26
Hatching Eggs

Every spring, Mom ordered 100 baby chicks from the local feed and seed store. The peeping, yellow chicks were shipped in a special box through the post office, and they always arrived safely. Approximately 75 of them were male and 25 were female. She raised the males for their meat and the females to become egg layers.

In addition to the chicks and hens at our farm, we had a long-legged rooster with a large, red comb. He liked to strut around the yard and chase my youngest brother, Dan. However, us older kids loved to tease the bird by chasing it and watch him run "like a chicken."

Occasionally, a small batch of chicks hatched at our farm. Mom had grown up learning German, the native language of her parents, and she called a setting hen a glucke. One day, I discovered a scraggly-looking hen sitting on a nest inside a large, wooden crate. I thought it was an unusual place for her to be laying eggs. I reached through the opening to get them; but she puffed up her feathers, tried pecking me and began making a strange clo-clo-clo noise. The hen didn't sound anything like our other chickens. When I asked Mom about the incident, her reply was, "She's a glucke. Leave her alone, because she's trying to hatch baby chicks from those eggs."

"How long does that take?" I asked.

"About 21 days," Mom answered. "Sometimes the eggs just rotten and boy do they stink! But if all goes well, we'll get some baby chicks."

Not long after that, we had fun watching the mother hen lead her little family around the farmyard. She was very protective of her offspring. It was kind of sad that the store bought ones never had the privilege of having such a caring mother. However, Mom did an excellent job of raising her flock of 100 chicks. It was rare that she would lose more than one or two of them.

Even though we lived on a farm, none of us kids ever saw an egg hatch. All that changed, though, one day at the country school where I was a fifth grader. We had about six assemblies each year, featuring touring performers or speakers. The cost was a dime. For this particular assembly, my parents chose not to give Delores, Tom or me money for the admission fee.

Typically, the students not attending the function were supervised by a teacher or the secretary. On this occasion, the secretary was in charge. She only had to watch the neighbor's four boys, Delores, Tom and me. We took our books upstairs to the fourth grade classroom. It was located right beside the office where the secretary was busy working. She trusted us to study on our own.

However, Ricky, the neighbor's son, ventured past the secretary to the first grade classroom. Upon his return, he excitedly announced that there was an incubator and a baby chick was hatching. We certainly didn't want to miss anything important like that! We asked the secretary for permission to watch the event, and she kindly said yes.

Our little group eagerly entered the dimly lit classroom. The teacher had shut off the overhead lights before going to the assembly. But it didn't matter, because we could see through the glass lid of the incubator. It was lit up by what we thought was just a big light. We were thrilled to see that one chick was in the process of hatching. We intently watched it peck through the thin shell at the larger end of the egg. It only had to peck a little further to complete a circle. Then to our disappointment the light suddenly went off, and it became fairly dark inside the incubator. We could still see the eggs, but the brightness had really showcased the hatching. Ricky reached over and turned on a knob. To our surprise, the bulb came on. He told us when he was in the room earlier he had figured out how it worked.

After what seemed like a long struggle, the white eggshell finally split in two. We had just seen something special happen right before our eyes! The newborn had ugly, wet feathers and appeared to be quite weak as it lay on the bottom of the incubator. It wasn't cute like the day old chicks Mom bought from the feed and seed store.

Our timing to watch the eggs hatch must have been perfect, for we noticed that a few more chicks were trying to "scramble" their way out of their shells. Every time the light went out, we turned the knob, forcing it come back on. Eventually, we grew bored with the first graders' project. We decided to go back to the fourth grade classroom where we did very little studying before the other students returned from the assembly.

The next day, my older sister Delores and I were in the same classroom even though she was a grade ahead of me.

Mrs. Dorsey taught a few subjects to a combined class of fifth and sixth graders. She sounded rather serious when she announced to the whole class that Delores and I were to report to the principal's office. It was a humiliating moment. As we walked upstairs, I asked, "What did we do wrong?"

"I don't think anything," Delores replied. When we entered the principal's office, familiar faces were there, namely our brother Tom and the neighbor's four boys. When I realized it was the exact same group of students who hadn't attended the assembly, a light bulb quickly lit up.

The principal sternly told the group that the first grade teacher was very upset with us. He informed us that every time we turned the knob the heat lamp had raised the temperature inside the incubator. We had innocently cooked her project and deprived the first graders of an educational experience.

I don't know if the students who were present at the assembly learned anything that day, but those who didn't attend it certainly did. We learned to keep our hands off of other people's property, or else something might "hatch out of a situation" that shouldn't.

27
Key of Trust

Living on a farm during the 50s, 60s, 70s and very early 80s was a down-to-earth experience for my brothers, sisters and me. Couple that with a more innocent time, and it isn't a wonder that the ten of us grew up to be very trusting.

Our parents demonstrated trust every time we left home. Since our farm was located a half mile from the nearest highway, we were rather isolated. Usually, the only people who ventured into our yard were those we were well acquainted with. If our neighbors happened to come over while we were away, Dad and Mom knew they were trustworthy. Thus, they saw no reason to ever lock our home and carry a house key with them when we were gone.

I do recall one time when we came home after a rain, and tracks were visible in our graveled yard. I detected a bit of concern in Mom's voice as she said, "I wonder who's been here." There was no note left at the door; therefore, we didn't have a clue who had been at our place. Thankfully, everything was exactly as we had left it.

Even after that incident, my parents continued to leave the house unlocked while we were gone. However, I do remember one time when the doors of our home were secured for a totally different reason. Dad was in the field working and Mom was shopping in town with a couple of her children. My oldest sister, Delores, was in charge, and she was being a bit bossy. After telling us in no uncertain terms that we were getting the house too messy, she chased us with the broom. We hurriedly ran outside to get away; but to our dismay, she locked the doors.

We thought she might not let us inside until Mom got home. Our situation seemed rather hopeless until Tom thought of an old, rusty key that we had seen stashed away in the car garage. We wondered if it would unlock either of the front doors of our house. It certainly would be worth a try!

Luckily, the key fit. However, we still had a problem. Delores was using her body to barricade the door. Finally, she conceded, giving the rest of us the feeling of victory. Tom returned the key to the car garage. We certainly wouldn't need it anytime soon unless our oldest sister decided to lock us out again.

I also remember a totally different situation when the locks on the doors gave my brother, sisters and me a real sense of security. It was a Sunday evening and our parents wanted to visit relatives who lived seven miles from us. Since us older kids had homework to do, we decided to stay at home. Besides, we felt like we had outgrown visiting relatives. The younger kids went along with Mom and Dad.

The sun had gone down, and the darkness of night had set in. We were sitting around the kitchen table with our books and papers spread out before us. All of a sudden, we heard a pounding noise. "It sounds like somebody is knocking on the door!" Patty exclaimed. We were all scared, but we took some comfort in knowing that the dog hadn't barked.

Everyone knew the smartest thing to do was check outside. Tom bravely led the way to the porch. His sisters timidly followed him. He flipped on the yard light, and nothing appeared out of the ordinary. Course, it was too dark for us to see off in the distance. Just to be on the safe side, we decided to lock both doors.

Back at the kitchen table, we tried to concentrate on our homework. A few minutes later, the same thumping noise scared us again. We glanced at each other fearfully. "I wish Dad and Mom were here," Patty said uneasily. Her eyes looked as big as silver dollars.

For a moment, we sat there in silence, trying to decide what to do next. We concluded that we'd done all we could by locking the doors. The dog still wasn't barking, so whatever made the noise couldn't be too dangerous. Still, it took us awhile to wind down from the adrenaline rush.

It was time to finish up our homework. Without thinking, I picked up my pencil. Its lead point was stuck in a large, blue eraser. I nervously tapped the rubber eraser on the table. As I did, a similar sound occurred. I continued tapping it and asked, "Was this the noise we heard?"

The others shook their heads in agreement. Even though we were nearly 100 percent sure that we had solved the mystery, we continued to feel uneasy. Our imaginations could still picture something lurking in the darkness. The doors remained securely locked until the rest of the family returned home. We sure were glad to see them! Like usual, when we went to bed that night, the doors weren't locked. Dad never saw any reason to do so.

My parents' trust was well-founded. In the 25 years that we lived on the farm, nothing was ever stolen. Course, as the decades have passed on by into a new century, times have changed considerably. Sadly, the "key of trust" has certainly gotten very rusty.

28
Favorite Milk Cows

The milk cows' supply of ground corn was getting low. So on a Saturday morning, Dad told his older kids, "Let's go grind some corn."

He parked the old blue truck under the grinder, drove his John Deere in place and put the belt around the tractor's flywheel and the shaft of the grinder. When everything was running, he joined Tom in the corncrib, and they began shoveling ears of dried corn into the hungry machine.

The assembly line system worked well for this job. Delores and Luke were stationed on the truck box where the ground up corn was being dumped. They filled milk buckets with the powdery feed and handed them down to Judy, Mary and me. We had to cross the corral fence and carry them a short distance into the barn. Patty was standing inside the granary, waiting to empty our pails.

Judy, Mary and I had to hustle back to the truck with our empty pails to keep everything moving along smoothly. It took awhile to grind a large batch of feed, but the cows always appreciated a satisfying meal while they were being milked by hand.

Before the evening milking, a couple of us kids had to herd them home. We'd leave the house around 4:30 p.m. It never seemed to fail that they would be grazing at the far end of the pasture, making it a long walk.

This time, it was Judy's and my turn to go after them. We separated out our six milk cows from the rest of the herd and were relieved when they cooperated and started heading for home. However, they were taking their sweet time, stopping to munch on grass every so often. We were well aware of the fact that any one of them could suddenly get stubborn and try running back to rejoin the rest of the herd. Then, our only option would be to pick up sticks or dead tree branches, which were scattered about in the pasture. We would yell plenty loud and use them as weapons to coax her to cooperate. If she didn't, she would be left behind to suffer the consequences. The next morning, she'd be eager to be milked.

On this evening, it didn't appear that any of the cows were going to give us trouble, though. They were approaching the big ditch that ran through the heart of the pasture. We called it the Number One. Quite a bit of water was flowing under the sturdy, wooden bridge that spanned the width of the ditch.

As the heavy cows crossed over the bridge, Judy and I listened to their hooves go, "Clompety, clomp…" The sound reminded us of the famous children's book, "The Three Billy Goats Gruff." Only their much smaller hooves went, "Trip, trap…" Unlike the fairy tale, we knew a nasty, old troll didn't live under the bridge. We had seen muskrats swim through the muddy water before, but that was about it.

Once we were on the other side of the bridge, the cows went over to the ditch for a drink of water. They tried to stay near the edge; but inevitably, their legs sank into some mud. When they turned and lifted their hooves, a sucking noise resulted.

The rest of the way home, the cows behaved themselves beautifully. They were in single file, following the trail that had been blazed many times before. By the time they reached the barn, those handling the milking chore were ready to get started.

Throughout the years, we had a bunch of milk cows, but a few of them became our favorites. Stinker, a Brown Swiss, was our smartest milk cow. She amazed everyone when she learned how to lift the hook on the gate and step inside the barn. She acted like a puppy dog following the person milking her over to the granary and reaching inside for a sneak bite. She also had a habit of eating her feed quickly, because she'd get seconds.

Obviously, Stinker had acquired her name because of her ornery behavior. One day, when Dad was unloading hay with his Farmhand, her eagerness got her into trouble. A sharp tooth of the Farmhand jabbed her in the side, causing a nasty-looking gash. Fortunately, the wound didn't get infected and healed up nicely without a veterinarian's attention.

Blackie, an Angus mix, was our largest milk cow. She was pure black and by far the best producer we owned. To us, she was like a gentle giant, but the other cows all respected her size. After having one of her calves, she got very sick. Dad called the vet, who gave her a shot for milk fever. Soon, she was back to her old self.

Little Red, like her name implied, was a petite Shorthorn. Thus, the other cows could easily boss her around. Routinely, she was the last one waiting in the corral for her turn to be milked. Her best trait was definitely her patience, which made her special. She seemed to have more of it than all of the other milk cows combined.

Since we dealt with our milk cows twice a day, they became like pets to us. I remember when Dad told the family Blackie was getting too old. She wasn't productive anymore, so she would be going to the sale barn the following Wednesday. When we asked Mom if another farmer would buy her, she shook her head and honestly replied, "She'll be butchered." Sadness filled our hearts, and we didn't want Wednesday to arrive.

But it did. Dad put the stock racks on the truck, and he coaxed the big, gentle cow up on the truck box. "Dan can go with me to the sale barn today," he said. His youngest son put on his ball cap and eagerly climbed into the cab.

The rest of the family watched as they pulled out of the yard. I'm sure we were all thinking about the same thing, "Poor Blackie. She won't be coming home." It was tough saying goodbye to one of our favorite milk cows. She'd been a part of our family for many years.

29
Beautification Campaign

As First Lady of our nation, Lady Bird Johnson focused a great deal of her time on making Washington, D.C., a more beautiful city. Because of her relentless efforts, it was cleaned up and lots of flowers, shrubs and trees were planted. While her beautification campaign was centered in the nation's capital, it was meant to be an example of inspiration to other cities across America.

I was in junior high when she was the First Lady. I remember how the students from our country school gathered in the cafeteria to watch a film on the subject of beautifying our country. The large, white screen was pulled down, and a teacher turned on the movie projector. As the black-and-white film began playing, it was accompanied by the loud, clear voice of the narrator. In the background was the soothing sound of the projector at work.

The message I got from the educational film was that tossing garbage out of a vehicle caused our roadways to look trashy. There were also too many billboards and junkyards next to our highways, giving them a cluttered appearance. The scenic view people saw as they traveled across the country was being destroyed. In other words, the First Lady was calling upon everyone to cooperate and preserve the beauty of the country we called home. As a united nation, we could make a difference.

I was 13 years old at the time. My family never went on vacation, so the only roads we traveled were close to home. But I had to agree that the ditches along those roadways were littered with trash. I recall sitting in the back seat of my parents' moving car and seeing someone in the vehicle ahead of us toss a full paper sack out of the window. The junk inside the bag was scattered about by the wind before it landed helter-skelter on the ground. There the garbage would remain for a long time unless someone made the effort to pick it up.

My husband Ben recalls how easy it was for him as a boy to find lots of empty pop bottles along the highway. That's because people had a bad habit of tossing them out of their car windows. It was the easiest, laziest way to dispose of them. He rode his bike along the edge of the paved road with a gunnysack hanging over the handlebars. As he combed the barrow pits, he found plenty of bottles that could be returned for a couple of cents each. Once his sack was full, the trip into town was rather difficult. The glass bottles clanked inside the heavy burlap bag. He turned them in at the local gas station for cash. With the money he earned, he purchased pop and candy. In his small way, he got a jump-start on the First Lady's beautification campaign.

I recall one solution that the film presented. Everyone should put a bag in the car, collect their junk in it and empty it at home. Businesses in the area did their part by handing out free ones for that very purpose. The small, plastic bags usually advertised their company. They had a hole at the top of them, so they could easily be hung on a radio knob, cigarette lighter or a window crank. Mom put one of those bags in our car, and we began using it. I also remember her saying that motorists who were caught littering would be fined. Even if there wasn't a cop in the area, our family felt guilty if we slipped back into our old ways and littered.

While law enforcement could only do so much; in my opinion, it was the First Lady herself who set up the biggest roadblock in curbing careless littering. Through education, she showed Americans how ugly their country was destined to look if it stayed on the same path. In the process, many citizens of this nation began complying with her wishes, and different attitudes soon became obvious.

Although it has been nearly a half century since I saw the film, the beautification message has remained with me today. There is no doubt that some parts of the United States are naturally more scenic than other places. However, whatever the appearance of the landscape, it always looks better uncluttered. So, why litter?

30
Dining
at A&W

My siblings and I never had to learn acceptable manners while dining inside a fancy restaurant, mainly because our parents never took us there. However, they probably had good reason not to. Occasionally on a Saturday or Sunday evening in the summer, Dad got a brave notion to take the family out to eat at A&W, a drive-in restaurant.

It was still hot outdoors as we pulled in the parking lot with the large orange, brown and white sign. The windows of our emerald green station wagon were all rolled down, because our car didn't have air conditioning. The fresh air felt good to us, but the people sitting in the cars right beside us probably wished we would have parked elsewhere. Judging by the looks we were getting, it could have been from the noise level we were creating, by how many of us were packed inside one vehicle or for both reasons.

Our station wagon had two seats facing forward, while

the third one faced the rear of the car. It was barely large enough to hold ten kids and two adults, but we managed to squeeze inside it. Course, once the food came, we would have a few more complications to deal with.

Before long, a carhop dressed in a uniform stepped up to Dad's window. She wrote down his hamburger order on a pad. She didn't seem surprised at the large number he'd requested. Perhaps it was because she saw lots of eyes staring at her. "Make those with the works...mustard, onions and pickles," he requested.

She asked if he wanted fries, and he replied, "No, but we need two large mugs of root beer and ten baby root beers." She jotted the information down before walking inside the restaurant to give the cooks the ticket she had completed.

For us kids waiting on the food seemed to take forever. We were definitely hungry and ready to eat. When we spotted two carhops approaching, excitement filled our vehicle. The one young lady put a tray of wrapped hamburgers on Dad's window, which was partially rolled down. She told him the price, and he handed her the cash. Meanwhile, the other gal positioned her tray that was filled with mugs of root beer on Mom's lowered window.

Dad handed the wrapped hamburgers back to my sister in the second seat. She in turn passed them out to waiting hands. Our mother carefully handed out the tiny mugs of root beer, which had a layer of white foam on top of them. She then gave Dad his adult-size mug of pop. The other large one was for Mom, and it remained on the tray beside her.

It was like a juggling act trying to eat a hamburger while holding onto the sturdy glass handle of the heavy cup. Sometimes we put our drink between our knees to hold it. The hamburger tasted good, but the root beer was delicious.

"I spilled some of my pop on the floor!" Jackie cried out. Mom grumbled before handing napkins to her. At that particular moment, she was probably wondering if it wouldn't have been easier just to cook at home. At least, there were plastic mats protecting the carpet underneath. Soon, the mess was wiped up as well as it could be.

It didn't take us long to devour the food and drinks we were given. Unfortunately, we were still hungry. After the empty mugs were piled onto the trays, Dad turned his headlights on. It was a signal to the carhop that she could pick up the trays. But before she carried them off, he made our day by ordering 12 small vanilla ice cream cones.

When they were delivered to our vehicle, Dad once again paid her, and she gave him change. As he handed them to eager hands, he instructed us, "Hurry up and eat them before they melt all over the place."

Dad pulled out of the A&W parking lot while us kids were busy licking the delicious swirled vanilla ice cream. Perhaps the people parked in the vehicles near us were glad that we were departing, but my siblings and I were just happy that we weren't going away empty-handed. The drive-in restaurant had given us a few extra napkins, and it was a good thing. Eating our dessert in a packed station wagon could easily become rather sticky situation for our family.

31
Manual Car Wash

In the 1960s, lots of automatic car washes were being installed across the United States. For many, being able to wash their vehicle mechanically was a welcomed convenience.

As a farm wife, Mom wasn't about to drive our station wagon 15 miles into Sterling and go through an automatic car wash. That would just be plain foolish! She'd done it the old-fashioned way for years, and she wasn't about to change now. If it was a hot day and she was in a car cleaning mood, she simply backed it out of the garage and parked the dirty vehicle under the shade trees. It was the coolest place for her to work.

There were several convenient things about Mom's manual method. She didn't have to wait for a bay to open up at the car wash, race against a timer or dig up enough change to finish the job. She simply gathered up her cleaning supplies and carried them outside.

First, the doors of the car were swung open, and the clear plastic floor mats were removed. Mom thoroughly rinsed them off at the pump house faucet and hung them on the clothesline to dry. She used a tiny brush to sweep up any debris on the carpets and washed the vinyl seats, door panels and dash of the car with a bucket of warm, soapy water.

After the inside was spic and span, Mom concentrated on the vehicle's outer appearance. The station wagon had picked up lots of dirt from our farm roads. She dipped her rag into the soapy water and scrubbed away the grime, working her way around the car. The excess water dripped to the ground. When she was ready to rinse off the soap, she went back into the house to get another bucketful of water. Since our well water was very soft and wouldn't leave spots, she was able to let it air dry.

The inside of the car's windows were just as dirty as the outside of them had been. As Mom wiped away fingerprints and erased smudges left by her children's foreheads or noses, the windows became crystal clear. The final step was to put the floor mats back in place and park the shiny vehicle in the garage. I remember it was a lot of work for Mom to give our car a bath the old-fashioned way, but the end result made it look almost brand new again.

Sunday evening, a few days after Mom had tidied up our car, Dad wanted to take a drive to the North Sterling Reservoir to see how much water was left in it. My siblings and I enjoyed going for drives, but the reservoir certainly wasn't our favorite place to go.

After traveling about 12 miles, we drove over a large hill and a portion of the reservoir came into view. To us kids it looked like a huge body of water, almost the size of the ocean. Dad followed a narrow, winding road that felt like we were climbing up a mountain. When he started driving slowly over the dam, we could all see the steep, rocky cliff on our left, and the wavy, dirty reservoir water on the right. "I don't want to go crashing down into the water, but the other side looks just as scary!" Mary exclaimed. She wasn't alone in her fear, because all of us kids were petrified of tumbling off of the dam to certain disaster below.

Dad didn't seem the slightest bit concerned about having an accident, though. His attention was focused on the water level. "It's really low," he commented to Mom. "Course, it's been a hot, dry summer, so what can you expect. I just hope we'll have enough irrigation water to get by. It certainly would help if we got a few good rains along the way."

Through the front windshield, we could see another vehicle approaching. Dad moved over near the edge and kept on driving slowly. The gravel road was barely wide enough for two vehicles to pass by one another, so us kids were relieved when Dad could once again drive down the middle of the roadway. The dam was nearly a mile long, and it seemed to take forever to cross over it. As I vividly recall, the best part about going over the barrier was when we finally exited off of it.

Dad then proceeded to drive around other sections of the huge lake where we saw campers, fishermen, swimmers, boaters and skiers. Everyone looked like they were having lots of fun. For my brothers, sisters and me, reservoir water didn't mean recreation. For us, it entailed work and plenty of it. Whenever we got water from the reservoir, we helped with the flood irrigating of our fields.

Our crops were getting dry, and it was time for Dad to place his next order. He turned onto the highway, drove a few miles and pulled into the ditch rider's yard. "I'm going to order three feet of water for Tuesday," he told Mom before going up to the door and knocking on it. Even though we had gotten a telephone recently, he still preferred to do his business face-to-face.

The ditch rider was in charge of keeping track of how much water we'd used out of our allotted rights and what we had left. Plus, it was his job to change the amount of water spilling into the outlet canal daily. In order to do that properly, he had to calculate the total number of feet requested by all of the area farmers.

It took Dad awhile to finish handling his business. In the meantime, my brothers, sisters and I didn't mind waiting out in our clean station wagon, which was parked on level ground. We were just happy, having survived another trip over the scary dam.

32
Cold, Soggy Fries

Quite often Mom made French fries and hamburgers for our noon meal, which we called dinner. Since she didn't have any fancy kitchen gadgets, she used a knife to peel the potatoes and slice them lengthwise to the proper size. She fried the potatoes in a pan of hot oil on her gas stove. Of course, when the fries were crispy and ready to take out of the bubbling oil, everyone had to be in the house prepared to eat. If not, they would quickly get cold, soggy and taste terrible.

Occasionally that presented a problem, because Dad never wore a wristwatch. He was good at relying upon the sun and his instincts to tell him when it was noon. But there were a few times when he got overly involved with his field work, and he failed to get home at midday. Back then, there weren't any cell phones to communicate with, so Mom couldn't call Dad and say, "Dinner's almost ready. You need to be home in five minutes."

I remember one instance when Mom and I looked out the window to see if he was still harvesting barley in the field behind our house. We quickly knew the answer for there was a large cloud of chaff and dust trailing the combine. "Joann, run out to the field and tell your dad it's time to eat," Mom said in an irritated tone. "The food will be on the table before he gets here."

A short while later, they entered the kitchen and Mom exclaimed, "It's about time you got here! The French fries probably won't be worth eating!"

Dad just smiled, shrugged his shoulders and replied, "The time just got away from me."

The fries were cold and soggy, but Dad didn't seem to mind. He was still busy thinking about his barley crop. When it got ripe enough to cut, he liked to get it harvested as quickly as possible. He knew from years of experience that every summer thunderstorm could contain devastating hail. It didn't take him long to devour his meal and head back out to the field.

"I'm surprised all of the French fries got eaten up," Mom said, sounding pleased. "At least, I didn't cook them for nothing."

Dad didn't make a habit of being late for dinner. In fact, it was generally the other way around. If he was scheduled to get irrigation water from the reservoir, he preferred to eat dinner around eleven o'clock. As a veteran farmer's wife, Mom knew we shared a main ditch with two of our neighbors. That ditch had a head gate with moveable boards. By adjusting them, Dad was able to control which way the water flowed. Therefore, he had to be up at the head gate when it arrived.

I recall one time Dad got a little more antsy than usual. Mom saw him drive into the yard and right away she guessed why. "He's home for dinner already! I haven't even started cooking, yet!" she stewed. But it didn't take her long to fix hamburgers and a bowlful of crispy French fries. Since we were eating an hour earlier than usual, nobody was very hungry.

Mom wasn't surprised that Dad quickly finished his meal and was raring to go. On this particular day, he chose Tom, Luke and Dan to go along and help him with the irrigating. However, they couldn't do anything but wait at the head gate until our water arrived, which was usually between noon and one o'clock.

Once that happened, it was time for the four of them to spring into action. It didn't take them long to get the water set and flowing down the corn rows. Irrigation water was usually in short supply, and Dad didn't want to waste any of it.

In the 32 years that my parents farmed, they always flood irrigated their crops. It was time-consuming work, and there were plenty of muddy canvasses to carry and lots of tubes to set. It just wasn't the boys who helped with the irrigating; the girls all had a wealth of experience in that area, as well.

While center pivot irrigation systems were a new way of watering crops, none of the farmers in our territory owned one. Thus, like Dad, they were quite dependent on the North Sterling Reservoir for their water supply.

33
Trading Stamps

L ike many women across America, Mom enjoyed saving and redeeming trading stamps. For them, it was a simple, fun way to get new merchandise and feel like they were getting it for free. Gas stations, grocery stores and various other businesses used the small paper coupons as a way to attract loyal customers. In reality, they had to raise their prices to support the marketing program.

Trading stamps reached the height of their popularity from the 1930s to the 1960s, but they continued on for a few more decades. The only business where Mom received stamps was at the grocery store. The one she preferred to shop at distributed stamps from the Gold Bond Company. After the groceries were rung up on the register, the cashier used an automatic dispenser to give out the appropriate number of gold-colored paper coupons based upon the total dollars spent. Since Mom usually bought a cartful, the employee neatly wrapped long ribbons of them around her hand. The large ones had a 10 printed on them, and they were worth ten times as much as the smaller stamps.

The grocery store was our last stop before heading home. After the sacks of groceries were put away, Mom asked my youngest sister Joann to paste the stamps in the small Gold Bond book. It was an enjoyable task, so she certainly didn't mind doing it.

The stamps were perforated so they could easily be torn apart. Joann licked a strip of the larger paper coupons and pasted them in the preprinted spaces down the middle of the page, making that one complete. When she was pasting in the smaller paper coupons, she had to fill in all of the preprinted rectangular spaces on the page to complete it. From past experience, I knew the more stamps she licked the drier her tongue got and the stronger the glue tasted.

The Gold Bond Company printed catalogs to showcase the premiums they were offering their customers. Mom had one of them to browse through. It told her how many books were needed to acquire a certain item. Since it took quite awhile to save up for the desired merchandise, we never made many trips into the redeeming store. It was an exciting day when we did go there.

This time Mary and Jackie got to accompany their mother into the store. Mom knew Betty, the friendly lady, who managed the place. While they got caught up on the latest happenings in their lives, the girls looked over the wide variety of merchandise that was displayed.

Mom didn't need to do that, because she already knew what she wanted to exchange her stamps for. The manager quickly thumbed through the sheets, making sure the correct amount of paper coupons was pasted on each of them. It was also part of her job to run the small booklets through a machine, which punched holes through the pages. The redeemed books fell through a slot into a clear plastic, sealed box below. It was a precautionary measure so no one could reuse them. Mom was thrilled to be leaving the store with a nice item without having spent a dime.

A couple of sports-related items that Mom got by exchanging stamps for them were a badminton set and a croquet set. They were games our whole family could participate in. She also got a very nice noodle cutter and a large ice chest that we took on picnics and to family reunions. Our parents likely wouldn't have splurged and bought any of those things, which they considered luxuries.

Later on down the road, the grocery store quit distributing Gold Bond stamps. Consequently, the redeeming store was closed. Fortunately for Mom and the other women in the area, their supermarket switched to another trading stamp company. They now lured customers in by giving the Mor-Valu brand. The larger ones were a bluish-green color and the smaller paper coupons were a pinkish-orange. The same lady who had managed the Gold Bond Store was now in charge of the new one.

In the early 80s, the local supermarket quit offering stamps altogether. The gift store remained open for a short period of time. It gave collectors one last opportunity to redeem those that they had meticulously saved. When Mom traded hers in, the manager told her lots of people were really upset that the program was being discontinued.

But end it did. Grocery stores began spending their marketing dollars on advertising lower prices instead of issuing stamps. Progress, more than likely, was part of that trade.

34
Baking from Scratch

While Mom was very busy mothering her flock of ten children, she still took the time to bake pies, cakes, strudels, doughnuts, etc., from scratch. She did it so often that we just expected those desserts.

Mom kept her flour in a canister in the kitchen; but when it was empty, she had plenty in reserve. Since we didn't have a pantry, she stored her big, black flour can in a rather unusual place. She kept it in the corner of her bedroom closet where it was almost hidden behind hanging clothes. The tall can had handles on each side and a lid, which sealed the top of it. The heavy-duty metal container had originally belonged to her mother. Even though it was old, it was still quite sturdy.

I enjoyed refilling the canister. After taking off the flour can's lid, the first thing I saw was an aluminum cup lying on top of the white powder. It was really an old drinking cup, but Mom had found a new use for it. I picked it up by the handle, dipped into the mound of flour and dumped the soft, fine baking ingredient into the canister.

Several times a year, Mom's flour supply would run low. It was time for her to make a trip to the local elevator in Sterling and buy some more. She liked to purchase it in either 25 or 50 pound sacks. She waited as an employee ground the wheat and bagged it in a good quality material.

After getting home, she dumped the essential baking ingredient into her black flour can. Back then, nothing was wasted. She washed the flour sack and recycled it by sewing it into tea towels or scarves. The tea towels did a wonderful job of drying dishes, and the scarves kept our heads warm while doing chores.

Throughout the years, I watched Mom make enough doughnuts to know her routine. First, she mixed up a big batch of dough and set it aside to rise. Later, she'd punch the air out of it, knead the elastic ball and cover it again. The yeast sprang into action one more time.

When the dough had finally reached the stage where it was time to roll it out, Mom spread a thin layer of flour on the kitchen table. I could tell she was applying pressure on the handles of the rolling pin, for it creaked and popped as the dough was being stretched out to the right thickness. Since she didn't have a store bought doughnut cutter, she improvised by using a glass coffee cup that had a broken handle. She inverted the cup and using wrist action firmly pressed into the dough. A circular pattern cut through to the table's surface.

Mom was also inventive when it came to her doughnut hole cutter. She opened the refrigerator, pulled out a bottle of ketchup and unscrewed the metal lid. She washed it and began pressing the white lid into the precut circles. As she did so, puffs of air escaped from the dough.

I wasn't the only one who liked to watch Mom bake.

This time, my youngest sisters Jackie and Joann were having a blast removing the small, sticky pieces of punched out dough. Occasionally, Mom saved a few of the round balls to fry into doughnut holes, but most of them were tossed back into her scrap pile. This, of course, was rolled out again and more doughnut shapes were cut out of it.

Meanwhile, a pan of oil was heating up on the stove. After it reached the right temperature, Mom carefully placed the raw, white dough into the sizzling oil. In no time at all, the doughnuts got puffy and began floating like boats. When the bottom side turned a nice brown color, she turned them over with a fork.

After the frying was completed, Mom made a simple glaze by dissolving powdered sugar in hot water. She dipped the fried doughnuts into the sweet, watery mixture and stacked them onto the same blue platter she always did. Although it wasn't labeled as our doughnut plate, it should have been. Just like it was only yesterday, I can still picture in my mind a mountain of those glazed doughnuts stacked on it.

A lot of times Mom made doughnuts when we were in school. Of all of my siblings, Delores was the one who loved to rush home after school and discover what, if anything, Mom had baked that day. "I smell homemade doughnuts!" she exclaimed as she burst through the kitchen door with her schoolbooks, and she was right! They were sitting on the kitchen counter just waiting for anxious young hands to grab one. We all loved their special, homemade flavor. Around our household, it didn't take long for them to disappear!

I can't imagine the number of hours Mom's work-worn hands spent baking desserts for her family from scratch. But I do know exactly how it feels to be blessed with a mother who lovingly did so. How "sweet" it was!

35
Picnic in a Pasture

Summer is the season when people gather outdoors to have a picnic. Typically, those outings take place in a park or someone's backyard.

My brothers, sisters and I thought we were really clever when we came up with an unusual setting for a picnic. We excitedly told Mom about our idea of having one in the pasture. She seemed rather skeptical and said that Dan was too young to go with us. He would have to stay at home with Dad and her, but the rest of us could have one.

So we eagerly began making plans. We could prepare the picnic lunch after church on Sunday morning. That would give us enough time to cook a homegrown fryer with Shake 'n Bake. We'd seen enticing commercials on TV advertising the product and were anxious to give it a try. It looked delicious and easy to make. All we would have to do was shake it and bake it. When we approached Mom with our main course idea, she suggested we pack some of the fried chicken that she would be making for their Sunday dinner instead. But we talked her into buying a package of Shake 'n Bake, which was a fairly new item at the grocery store.

On the morning of our picnic, Delores and I followed the directions on the package. Mom just shook her head as we made a mess in her kitchen. Still, we felt confident that the new food was going to turn out wonderful.

While the chicken was baking, Patty, Judy and Mary boxed up the rest of the food that we would be taking on our picnic. I don't recall what else was on the menu, but it surely had to include something sweet like cookies or candy bars. We probably took a bag of potato chips, too. Of course, we needed to take along something to drink and that was either lemonade or Kool-Aid. After it was mixed, the liquid was poured into the jug that we used when working in the field.

Once the chicken was finished baking, Delores, Tom, Patty, Judy, Luke, Mary, Jackie, Joann and I excitedly gathered up our picnic supplies and headed for the pasture. We brought along an old blanket to spread out on the ground. Tom and Luke carried a bat, softball and gloves. A ball game was one activity that we had planned on playing in the afternoon.

As the nine of us searched for the perfect picnic site, we continued to walk. We finally selected a spot near the south end of the pasture. It was far enough away from our house and a cluster of Russian olive trees would provide needed shade.

Not long after arriving at our destination, we decided to eat. Everyone gathered around on the blanket and the food was dished up. The chicken was still warm and it tasted okay. However, in our opinion, it certainly wasn't as good as the commercials made it appear. Actually, we missed the crispiness of the fried chicken Mom had raised us on.

However, we weren't planning on telling her that, because she would likely say, "I told you so."

During lunch, we noticed that our herd of cattle was slowly grazing closer to our picnic site. Perhaps it was their daily routine, or they were just curious about what we were doing. Understandably so, for they'd never seen people "eat out" in their territory before.

After everyone was finished eating, we were anxious to play a game of softball. We divided up into teams and agreed to make first base a tree. Second and third bases were actually a couple of old boards that we found in the pasture and home base was a fence post. It didn't take us long to figure out that the catcher had the worst position on the team. If he or she missed the ball, the only way to retrieve it was to crawl under the fence or straddle the sharp-pointed wires.

To complicate matters more, we were also playing near a deep ditch called the Number One, which etched its way through our pasture. On that particular summer afternoon, it was near full capacity. None of us could swim and since Jackie and Joann were still fairly young, we had to keep our eyes on them.

The cattle presented another problem, because they were grazing into our batting range. We didn't want to hit one of them with a fly ball or a grounder. Playing softball just wasn't working out like we thought it would. We finally gave up and decided to explore our surroundings.

Luke spotted a large, dome-shaped nest in one of the Russian olive trees. It was constructed mostly from sticks and didn't look like any nest that we'd seen before. After further inspection, we guessed that it might belong to a magpie. Unfortunately, the bird wasn't home, so we couldn't pester it.

We looked around our surroundings for another adventure. Tom came up with the idea that we should cross the barbed-wire fence and explore the neighbor's land. We were well aware of the fact that Dad wouldn't like us trespassing, but curiosity won out. Soon, we were running around in the neighbor's alfalfa field as free as butterflies. We also scurried through his dry irrigation ditch like squirrels and inspected the underside of a bridge. All the while, we kept a close eye out for the neighbor. If we saw him approaching, our plan was to rush back into our pasture. We'd then act as if we had been on our side of the fence all along. There was no reason to worry, for he was nowhere in sight.

Eventually, we decided to cross back over the fence into our property. Patty suggested that we walk across the gas pipeline, which spanned the width of another big ditch in our pasture. A sign was posted nearby warning us about the danger of gas, but we paid no attention to it. The trench was about eight feet deep. There was very little water in it, but there was plenty of stinky mud to fall into. Thus, the challenge we had been searching for.

Judy was the first brave one to step out onto the large, circular pipe and carefully balance her way across the ditch. Mary was the next one to accomplish the stunt. With a little practice, all of us older kids were soon maneuvering our way across the ditch rather quickly. Since Jackie and Joann were too young to balance themselves, Delores and I helped them scoot over the warm, black pipeline.

About mid-afternoon, we were all picnicked out. We picked up the blanket that had dried blades of grass stuck to it, bundled up our dirty dishes, ball equipment and headed for home. When we walked into the house, we noticed that Mom had already washed the dinner dishes. We sheepishly piled our dirty ones on the counter, hoping she wouldn't notice.

Rarely did our parents only have one kid at home, so we were fairly certain that we'd been missed. On the other hand, they might have enjoyed the peace and quiet. Either way, all nine of us were back after enjoying a fun-filled picnic in our pasture, featuring Shake 'n Bake chicken.

36
Scars from the Past

The way I remember iodine is that it stung a lot when the antiseptic was put on a cut or an abrasion. It came in a small, dark brown glass bottle. When the cap was unscrewed, there was a glass tube attached to it. We applied the liquid by rubbing the end of the tube, which had a small hole in it, over an open wound. The iodine discolored our surrounding skin and dried a rather ugly, yellowish-brown color.

Fortunately, my brothers, sisters and I only suffered minor injuries while growing up on the farm. We did get ourselves into quite a few predicaments where the outcome could have been much worse, though. We never thought a thing about using iodine on our wounds until one day when we were visiting our aunt and uncle's farm. One of our cousins cut his hand, and his mom applied some Mercurochrome on it. We had never heard of that medicine before, but we were certainly intrigued when the skin around his gash turned the prettiest, pinkish-red color. After he informed us it never stung even the tiniest little bit, we were sold!

As we were driving home, us kids told Mom about the pretty-colored medicine that didn't sting. The whole purpose of the conversation was to convince her to buy a bottle of Mercurochrome, so we wouldn't have to use iodine anymore. She didn't hesitate to inform us that iodine was the better medicine. Nor did she give any indication it was even a debatable matter when she posed a question in her response, "If it doesn't sting, how can it do any good?"

Accidents do have a way of happening even while doing routine activities. My siblings and I had just finished hoeing the garden, something we did quite often during the summer months. Patty and I decided to race the quarter-of-a-mile home on our bikes. It was going to be a challenge balancing our hoes on our handlebars, but my younger sister and I felt confident that we could do it. We agreed to hang them up in the machine shed where they were typically stored and race into the house. The first one there would be the winner.

Patty chose one side of the road created by the tires of our vehicles, and I was going to ride on the other well-worn path. We were soon pedaling our fastest. As we rounded the corner by the machine shed, both of us jumped off of our bikes at nearly the same time. It was a close competition, but luckily I was able to hang up my hoe just a split second before she did. There wasn't a doubt in my mind that I was going to be victorious. The homestretch was in sight!

As I hurried out of the machine shed, I tripped over the cement foundation. My right forearm was scraped by some rusty nails that were protruding from the side of an unfinished wall. The race was over. Patty came up to see how badly I was injured. I could tell by the sympathetic look in her eyes, she didn't think it was a pretty sight. Two nails had ripped through my skin like butter and had dug into the flesh. The deep scratches were about four inches long and were starting to bleed.

I panicked and ran into the house to show Mom. She immediately washed off the injured area in the bathroom sink and dried it with a towel. Her next move was predictable. She opened the medicine chest and pulled out the dreaded bottle of iodine. I didn't even resist, realizing the nasty-looking wounds needed something strong to help them heal. As she applied the antiseptic, it burned like fire. Suddenly, I got light-headed and my stomach became queasy. "I don't feel good," I mumbled.

"You better lay down," Mom replied, helping me over to the bed.

When I began to feel better, the bike race no longer seemed the slightest bit important to me. Mom then covered the ugly, yellowish-brown area with gauze and taped the bandage in place to prevent dirt from getting into it. The deep scratches did heal but not without leaving behind a pair of long, very noticeable scars on my forearm.

Many times when my siblings or I were injured, Mom would be firm about treating the wound with Lysol, which came in a dark brown bottle. She had a chipped, white porcelain enamel bowl she always used specifically for that purpose. She poured a small dose of the disinfectant into some water that she had heated up. We soaked the injury in the diluted solution for as long as we could stand it. The home remedy was quite painful, but it did cure an infection.

Back then, we didn't visit the doctor very often. Mom treated our injuries the best way she knew how with iodine or Lysol. My brothers, sisters and I all have our share of scars that happened while growing up on the farm. Fittingly, there is a story behind each of them that remains embedded in our minds today.

37
Cleaning Up
the Farmyard

O ne summer evening, Grandpa came out to our farm to visit. After getting out of the car, he told us kids, "You should clean up the yard." We didn't exactly like his comment, but it did take root.

My brothers, sisters and I spent a lot of time playing under the rows of elm trees, which surrounded our farmhouse on the west and north sides. Grandpa's remark was the reason we started noticing just how many small branches, sticks, twigs and pieces of tree bark had fallen to the ground from past windstorms. Delores, our oldest sister, mentioned how much neater the area would look if it was cleaned up. Rarely did we volunteer to work; but on that occasion, we got excited about doing so.

Since we lived on a farm, we never had a trash service that would come by on a periodic basis to pick up what we gathered. Then again, we were free to burn out in the country, so we asked Mom where we could stack the garbage we collected. She seemed delighted that we were ambitious and showed us where the debris should be piled in our graveled yard. "When you're finished, I'll come out and burn it," she informed us.

Busy as beavers, we worked together as a group. Delores raked the mess into small piles, while Patty, Mary, Jackie and Joann picked up the tangled rubble with a scoop shovel. The rest of the team carried the filled cardboard boxes over to the growing pile. To keep things fair, we traded jobs with each other every so often.

When the newness of the task wore off, we realized that we might have embarked on a bigger job than we'd originally thought. As we looked down the three rows of trees to see how far we had cleaned, it didn't look like much compared to the distance we still had to go. It was probably a good thing that sprucing up the area under the tree rows had been our idea rather than a task our parents had assigned us. We couldn't complain about the pickle we'd gotten ourselves into. Besides, the finished area looked so much neater that it inspired us to continue working.

Just before noon, we reached our goal. The area under the tree rows was tidy, and we felt really good about our accomplishment. We admired the large pile of trash that was stacked in the yard. It was amazing how much we had collected in a few hours. Unfortunately, Delores mentioned how dirty the rest of our yard now looked. My siblings and I came to an agreement that we'd tackle that task in the afternoon.

We were glad when Mom called us in for dinner, because we were starved. At the table, our parents expressed how pleased they were with our enthusiasm to continue sprucing up the place. They agreed that there were plenty of other things lying around the farmyard, which could also be burned.

After dinner, Dad went back out to the field, and Mom helped us. We split up and searched for garbage around the garage, boxcar, chicken house, brooder house, barn, pump house and corrals. We found rotten boards, ripped gunnysacks, scraps of cardboard, etc. and carried it to the yard where we pitched the junk onto the growing mound. Then, we went back for more.

About mid-afternoon, our mother decided to light the dry debris on fire. Us kids stood nearby and watched it go up into fiery flames. Mom had the responsibility of making sure our bonfire stayed under control.

By evening, our pile of garbage had been reduced to only black ashes. My siblings and I were glad that we had persisted with our efforts to clean up the yard when we could have easily become "burnt out" with the project. Instead, it became a different, almost fun day for us.

Trash wasn't the only unsightly mess around our farmyard. There were also lots of weeds seemingly growing by leaps and bounds. When they got tall and thick, Dad made the decision it was time to do something about them. He knew our cattle liked eating weeds. He'd observed them trying to reach over, under or through barbed-wire fences to snip them. Thus, it stood to reason that they would be the answer to this problem. But it was going to take everyone in the family to keep the cattle inside the areas they were allowed in and out of the place that were off-limits.

So on a nice summer evening, we chased the cattle out of the pasture and directed the herd to the area behind our garage. This is where our biggest weed problem existed. The trouble was our cellar was also located there. Mom was afraid that one of the cows would step on the roof, which was covered with dirt and weeds, and fall through. Therefore, Tom, Luke and Dan were stationed there, guarding the cellar area closely.

Once the antsy herd got over the fact that they were free to roam, they settled down and eagerly began grazing on the tall weeds and wild grass. With the cattle wandering about, the spaciousness of our large farmyard seemed to shrink considerably. It was amazing how quickly the cows and calves were mowing down those weeds! It was like inviting a threshing crew over to help with harvest.

The job was getting done very quickly with no thanks to Charlie, our bull. Judy was stationed on top of our small corncrib that was near our barn. Charlie thought the ears of corn looked much more appealing than the weeds did. He invited himself over to the crib. As the guard on duty, Judy bravely reached down and smacked him with a board. To her surprise, this never seemed to faze him. But when she slapped him with a belt, he noticed!

After the cattle had grazed around our yard for several hours, the light of day was beginning to fade away. Therefore, it was time for our family to work together and coax the herd back into the pasture.

The cattle being loose on purpose had been such a successful method of cleaning up our weeds that it became a summer tradition for our family. As I recall, my siblings and I only spent one of our days on the farm cleaning up the yard and watching the large pile of trash go up in smoke. But that bonfire was a memorable one!

38
When Sundays Were Special

Do you remember when Sundays were treated as a day of rest, and they had a totally different flavor than the other six days of the week? I do, because my parents instilled in us kids the value of keeping Sunday a holy day. Living on the farm, we couldn't avoid doing chores. Just like any other day of the week, the livestock needed attention. After doing them and eating breakfast, we dressed for church and made the 15-mile trip into Sterling.

On our way home from church, it seemed strange driving down Main Street. Traffic was very light, and there weren't any vehicles parked in front of the businesses. Downtown looked deserted, because all of the stores, gas stations, restaurants, etc. were closed for the day and would reopen on Monday morning. Thus, people had to think ahead and buy food, gas or whatever supplies they might need on Saturday for the following day. Traditionally, the noon meal on Sunday was considered to be the best one of the week. The main course often featured something special like fried chicken or pot roast with all the trimmings.

Our Sunday afternoons were spent in various ways. Occasionally, Mom was invited to a bridal shower, and she'd take one of her seven daughters and a gift for the bride-to-be. This time, I was the lucky one who got to go along with her, and next time it was going to be my sister Joann's turn.

The shower began with the introduction of the bride and her attendants. Then the guests were asked to stand up and introduce themselves to the group, which was rather embarrassing for me.

The majority of the afternoon was spent playing bingo. The winners from each of the games got to choose from an assortment of small, wrapped gifts. When the bingo cards were picked up, paper and pencils were passed out for another game. This one was designed to see who knew the bride the best. A series of questions were asked about her favorite things, and the guest coming up with the most correct answers won the prize. After that, one of hostesses asked, "Who's been married the longest?" Everyone immediately looked at the older women in the room. I was amazed that several of them had been married 50 plus years. The lady who spoke up with the highest number was given a special present.

It was then the bride's turn to become the center of attention. She opened the gifts that were stacked on a long table and announced who the packages were from. Most of the presents were practical things needed to set up a household such as towels, sheets and pillowcases, toaster, mixer, iron, etc. She thanked everyone for their generosity and invited them to stay for refreshments.

The hostesses served cake, punch and my favorite thing was the miniature paper cups filled with a mixture of nuts and colored mints. After everyone was through eating, they asked the guests to check the bottom side of their paper plates. The woman or girl with an "x" marked on it won the door prize. With that, the bridal shower was over, and Mom and I headed home. We hadn't won a thing, but it still was fun.

A lot of times relatives drove out to our farm to visit us on Sunday afternoons. If we didn't get company, we often turned on the TV and entertained ourselves with a ball game. Depending upon the season, we enjoyed watching baseball, football or basketball. My siblings and I and sometimes Dad also spent many hours playing our version of those three games out in our farmyard.

Occasionally on a lazy Sunday afternoon in the wintertime, Dad suggested that we play Ping-Pong. We had a net, a couple of paddles and Ping-Pong balls, but we didn't own a table designed specifically for that game. So we scooted our metal kitchen table out to the middle of the floor and moved the chairs into the living room. The kitchen was too small to be a recreational area, but it was the best place we had.

In the first game, Dad played Luke. After winning that match, he took on Dan as an opponent. Again, he was victorious. Then, the rest of us kids got our chance to join in on the fun. Given the fact that there were so many competitors, lots of different matchups were possible. We played until it was time to do the evening chores.

Mom usually fixed a simple supper on Sunday evenings since she claimed no one was very hungry anyway. A memorable food she made was Chef Boy-Ar-Dee Pizza. Everything was provided in the kit. All she had to do was add water to make the crust, top it with a can of Italian pizza sauce, sprinkle on the powdery cheese and bake it.

There wasn't any meat or vegetable toppings on the pizza, but it definitely had a unique taste.

Come Monday morning, the activity around our farm picked up immensely. When school wasn't in session, us kids helped our parents in whatever way we could during the week. After six work-filled days, our family welcomed a day of rest.

Somewhere along the way, times began to change. A few stores started opening up for business on Sundays, which meant employees had to work. It might not have been their choice, but it was required of them. At first, it seemed foreign for people to go shopping on Sundays, but it soon became routine. The new trend was catching on, and managers of other stores noticed. Thus, they had to be open, too. How else were they going to capture those dollars?

Little by little, Sundays began to blend in with the other six days of the week, making them lose their laid-back atmosphere. And along the way, something special was lost.

39
Migrant Workers

For six seasons, the same family of migrant workers came to our farm to work in our sugar beet fields. Their home base was in Texas, and they usually arrived about the first part of May. Andrew, Flora and their three young children Arturo, Freddie and Alicia lived in our beet labor shack until mid-July. They then traveled to Florida where they picked strawberries before returning to Texas.

When they arrived that first spring, they drove into our yard in an old car. They introduced themselves, and Dad showed them the shack where they'd be staying. It was located about a football field away from our farmhouse. It wasn't the nicest place to set up housekeeping, but Flora made the best of it. The small shack had two bedrooms and a kitchen/living room. It was furnished with the basic living necessities and electricity. Since it didn't have running water, they had to walk a short distance over to our pump house to get their water supply. Their bathroom facility was located nearby in the form of a faded, red outhouse.

My siblings and I were curious about our new neighbors. We quickly found out their kids weren't nearly as shy as us. They bravely ventured over into our yard, wanting to play. At first, we didn't know how to handle the situation, but it didn't take long until we began making friends with them.

Dad knew Andrew and Flora wouldn't get many beets worked with three young children out in the field. So he generously volunteered Mom to baby-sit them while the parents were working. As I recall, she was rather upset with him. "Just what I need, more kids!" she exclaimed. The only consolation in the deal was that Mom's older kids were busy working beets in another field. So during the days, she just had her younger children to watch, plus theirs. Still, that was plenty! However, Mom soon mellowed. She enjoyed giving Arturo, Freddie and Alicia cookies, which they really liked.

One afternoon, my younger brother Luke was playing with Arturo by our beet planter. They wanted to chop off a small tree branch with the row marker. So Luke untied it, and the sharp disk blade came slashing down and hit Arturo on the head. Mom was upset when she saw the deep gash on the young boy's scalp. She quickly placed a wet washcloth on the bleeding injury, got Arturo in our car and hurriedly drove out to the field to tell his parents. Andrew and Flora weren't angry; they realized it was just an accident. The couple decided to continue working while Mom took their son to the emergency room where our family doctor stitched him up.

Flora had no choice but to toil long, hard hours along-side her tall, slender husband. First, they thinned the extra beets out of the rows and later on they went through the fields again and hoed out those persistent weeds. Manual labor was the only way they knew how to make a living. Dad was quite pleased with their performance. He said they did an excellent job and were fast workers.

On one occasion, Dad sent his daughters Patty and Judy out to help Andrew and Flora. While they were working together, the couple taught them how to count in Spanish. My two sisters enjoyed the foreign language lesson.

Andrew and Flora expressed many times how much they appreciated working and living at our farm. They always called Dad, "Mr. Marcus." He didn't seem to mind one bit that they added mister in front of his first name. It was their way of showing respect for their boss.

Through the years, the Texas couple warmed up to Mom, too. When she gave birth to her tenth and last child named Dan, they made a surprise visit to the hospital. They gave a lovely glass flower arrangement as a gift.

Mom was also surprised when Flora came over to our house and invited my brothers, sisters and me to Freddie's birthday party. She mentioned that some of their relatives and friends were also invited. They were migrant workers, too, living about an hour away from our farm. Mom accepted the invitation on our behalf, but my siblings and I felt like we'd be outsiders at the social event.

On Sunday afternoon just before the birthday party was to begin, we got company. We thought Mom would allow us skip the party, so we could play with our cousins. That wasn't going to be the case, though. She insisted it would be rude if we didn't attend. My siblings and I reluctantly walked toward the shack. A large group of people were gathered outdoors, and we shyly approached them. Andrew greeted us and introduced us to their other guests.

It was perfect summer weather to have a birthday party outdoors. Flora had baked a beautiful white cake, and she gave us each a piece along with a scoop of ice cream. The cake was delicious, but my sister Judy didn't care for the pineapple ice cream at all. She tried slipping it under a log for the ants to eat, but she got caught! Flora wasn't angry; she just smiled, realizing pineapple wasn't her favorite flavor of ice cream.

Later, a mostly pink piñata became the center of attention. My siblings and I had never seen one before, so we definitely knew it was part of their Mexican culture. It was made out of papier-mâché and looked kind of like a horse. The pretty piñata was hung up on a tree branch out of reach. Flora told us that when it was our turn to swing at the piñata with a stick we'd be blindfolded. She also informed us the object of the game was to bust it open, because lots of candy was inside.

My siblings and I soon found out it was challenging. Consequently, everyone got several turns before someone finally broke it. The adults clapped and cheered while us kids hurried to grab our share of the sweets. The piñata was a new experience for my brothers, sisters and me, and we thought it was great. By the time the party was over, we were glad we went.

Over the six beet-working seasons that the Texas family worked at our farm, a trust and friendship definitely developed both ways. We were disappointed when they didn't return one spring. Our farm just didn't seem the same without them. Mom and Dad speculated that they had found work elsewhere. Since we had no way of contacting them, our family never found out the reason why; but we hoped all was well with them.

40
Autograph Book

For many years, autograph books were popular with young girls. The trend began changing when high school students, boys and girls alike, began signing school yearbooks.

In 1964, I was attending junior high at a country school. At that time, autograph books were at the tail end of being in style. To me, it seemed like every girl my age had one. I naturally wanted to be just like them and was thrilled when Mom surprised me with my very own book. Its shiny, slick cover was pinkish-purple and an assortment of blank colored pages was inside, waiting to be filled.

It only seemed fitting that Mom should be the first person to share some thoughts or wishes with me. "Will you write in my autograph book?" I asked. She seemed hesitant, but she saw the hopefulness in my eyes. So she sat down at the kitchen table and thought for awhile before writing in it.

Come Monday, I eagerly asked my friends, classmates and teachers to write in my personal book. When it was returned to me, I searched through the pages looking for the last entry. I was always curious what it said. Most everyone wrote sentimental or silly poems followed by their signatures.

Whenever relatives came out to our farm to visit, I'd ask them if they'd write something in my autograph book. My uncle just shook his head and said he wasn't very good in English class. Consequently, I didn't persist with the issue, but I was thrilled when two of my aunts complied with my wishes. Even Grandpa took the time to jot down several thoughts meant specifically for me. As I recall, he wrote some words of wisdom in English and a few sentences in German, which was his native language. I had to ask him what the foreign words meant.

Today, it would be fun to reread what others composed in my autograph book. I'm sure there were probably a few roses are red, violets are blue poems included in it. But somewhere, somehow my personal treasure was lost.

Remarkably, my mother-in-law's autograph book, which she received on March 1, 1935, was safely passed down to me. It had survived the test of time in good condition. The maroon cover and filled pages were bound together with a single ribbon.

As I thumbed through hers, many of the poems were unfamiliar to me. I noticed that girls, boys, teachers and relatives alike took a few moments of their time to respond to the question, "Will you write in my autograph book?" Here are some of their creative responses:

You ask me to write,
What shall it be?
Just two little words,
Remember me.

Flowers may wilt,
Birds may die,
Friends may forget,
But never will I.

In your chimney of friendship,
Count me as a brick.

Roses are red,
Violets are pink.
If you'd wash your feet,
They wouldn't stink!

The ocean is wide,
The valley is deep.
My love for you
Will always keep.

Remember well and bear in mind,
A nice young man is hard to find.
So when you find one handsome and tall,
Hang onto his shirttail summer and fall.

After the party's over,
Don't linger at the gate.
Love may be blind,
But the neighbors ain't.

When you get married and have twins,
Come over to my house for safety pins.

When you get old
And cannot see,
Pick up your specs
And think of me.

When the golden sun is setting,
And the path you no more trod;
May your name in gold be written,
By the autograph of God.

Even though the colored pages have faded with age, the freshness of simpler times continues to shine through in the messages written nearly 80 years ago.

41
Outhouse Bridges the Gap

O riginally, we had two outhouses on our farm. The one used by our family was located near the chicken house, and the other was conveniently placed close to the shack for our beet laborers' benefit.

In 1959, the landlord updated our farmhouse by installing running water and adding on a bathroom. Since our outdoor facility was no longer needed, Dad tore down the tiny building.

My early childhood memory bank doesn't recall much about having to use an outhouse as a bathroom. I do, however, distinctly remember when inclement weather prevented us from making the trip outdoors. An old five-gallon bucket was brought into our porch. The makeshift toilet was uncomfortable, and it smelled bad. On those occasions, the outdoor facility probably seemed like a luxury that had been taken away.

The beet laborers' outhouse survived extinction, because

it was still being used by them several months out of the year. Lucky for me, our seasonal help wasn't around when I came up with an entirely different way to keep it from sitting idle.

My early adolescent years had arrived, and there wasn't a doubt in my mind that I was getting quite grown-up. Certainly more so than Mom thought! I wanted to wear a bra to school like the rest of the girls in my class. They had all progressed to that stage, and I yearned to be the same as them; but Mom saw no reason to take me shopping.

However, my imagination would change the course of those confusing growing pains. Why, I had an older sister who had several old bras in her dresser drawer that she no longer wore. I saw no reason that I shouldn't, and more importantly couldn't, start wearing them. The next problem I faced was a bedroom full of sisters. We had to share the room, because the house wasn't large enough for such a big family. There would be no privacy dressing in my (our) room. I also realized if any of them found out about my new development in life, they would tease me endlessly. The deserted outhouse seemed like the perfect solution.

The next school morning, I dug out a bra, hid it in my pocket and went for a short walk to the forlorn outbuilding. I opened the rickety door, stepped inside and made sure it was latched. I could see the outside world through the cracks in the walls. Thankfully, there wasn't anyone around. I quickly changed into my grown-up girl apparel. Though the dressing room was not as fancy as those in clothing stores, it had served a purpose. I was now truly ready to go to school, and once there I felt like I'd crossed over a major threshold.

After school each day, I made another trip to the vacant outbuilding. This time the bra came off, was hid in my

147

pocket and returned to the dresser drawer. Who could possibly suspect anything unusual was going on in my life?

The visits to the outhouse went smoothly for awhile. That is until Mom embarrassed me by saying she was aware of the fact that I'd been wearing a bra. I was shocked that she knew, wondered how she found out about my secret, but was way too uncomfortable to ask any questions. The good that did come out of my imaginative solution was that Mom said, "Well…if you want to wear one that bad, I guess you can whether you need to or not!"

Most people think of an outhouse as being a private place; and in that respect, I agree with them. However, I doubt many young girls have ever made a personal dressing room out of one while they "bridged the gap" from childhood to womanhood.

42
Manual Typewriters

Memories from the past can be triggered by all of our senses. Such was the case when I was watching a television commercial recently, and I heard a crisp sounding, "Ding!" It instantly reminded me of the warning bell, which chimed when typists neared the right margin of manual typewriters. It alerted them that they might have to hyphenate a word, because only five spaces remained on that line. With a swish of the carriage return, the roller dropped the paper down one space.

The memorable sound had unexpectedly transported me back to my high school typing class. It felt like 1970 again, and I was a senior at Iliff High School. Our small class of 21 met in the downstairs typing room. It wasn't located near another classroom, probably for good reason. When everyone started pounding on the keys, we made quite a racket.

The first lesson the instructor gave us was to type ff, jj, ff, jj repeatedly with our index fingers. When the teacher thought we had learned those two homeroom keys, we began practicing on another couple of letters. Of course, each key we learned required a slightly different fingering technique. We were taught the entire keyboard in this manner. I thought the lessons seemed too simple and rather silly. Unfortunately, like everything else in school, the work became progressively harder the further we got into the course.

It soon became apparent to me that rhythm was very important. If I accidentally struck two keys simultaneously, they jammed up near the roller. That was very frustrating, because it took time to separate them.

Our timed drills only lasted for three or five minutes, but they were tough on the nerves. It felt like the start of an important race when the instructor said emphatically, "Go!" The noise level in the room instantly intensified, and my heart seemed to be beating faster than my fingers were typing. When I sensed that I had made an error, it caused me to temporarily lose my concentration. As the stopwatch ticked away, I began anticipating the teacher telling us to stop. At the end of the drill, we figured up the number of words per minute (wpm) that we'd typed and how many errors we had made. Typically, I typed between 35 and 40 wpm. For the most part, my results weren't much better than the boys in the class, but they were noticeably lower than the girls' scores.

At the time, I never thought of the following reasons or perhaps excuses for being a slow typist. Since I milked several cows by hand each day, my hands had become very muscular. I also had short, stubby fingers, so they had to stretch to reach the top row of keys. The other girls in my class had more ladylike hands, and most of them were promoted to an electric typewriter. Since we had a limited number only the best typists got one, and the rest of us remained on the manual style.

Our teacher only allowed us to use typewriter erasers to correct our errors. It was hard to erase the black ink off of the paper and make it look neat. I quickly learned not to press too hard or else my copy grew thin or got a hole in it.

To my dismay, I graduated from high school with a poor typing grade. Stubborn or foolish, whichever might fit best, I enrolled in a secretarial science program at the local junior college in the fall. The school of higher education only had electric typewriters. and the keys were much more sensitive. After getting used to that, my speed began to improve rapidly. There is a saying practice makes perfect. When it comes to typing, it definitely helps if your brain and hands are working in unison.

While at college, I was able to acquire a work-study job. I worked a few hours each week between classes in the agricultural division, which fit my farming background perfectly. I got to experience typing up tests on a master that acted similar to carbon paper. As the keys hit the two-part master, the colored wax from the second sheet was transferred onto the back side of the first page. The secretaries showed me how to correct an error by using a razor blade to scrape away the unwanted wax and then retype it.

Once I had finished typing the test, they taught me how to tear off the top copy, fasten it to the drum of a Ditto machine with the back side facing out. After turning on the machine and inverting the solvent container, it was time to print. As the drum spun, a strong-smelling alcohol was spread across each sheet by an absorbent wick. It dissolved the colored wax that contained ink and transferred the familiar light purple print onto the copies. While the test papers were slightly damp and limp, they had a faint sweet aroma.

Typically, the agricultural secretaries typed more important documents on a stencil, which was a flimsy, waxed sheet with a stiff card stock backing. The two sheets were bound together at the top. The typewriter ribbon had to be disabled, so that the typing element hit the stencil directly and cut it. Mistakes were corrected by brushing a special correction fluid over them; and when it dried, the text could be retyped.

After the document was typed, the template was wrapped around a bulky Mimeograph machine that had an ink-filled drum. Single sheets of paper were drawn through the rotating drum and the pressure roller. Black ink was forced through the holes of the stencil and onto the copies.

Both of these methods for producing copies eventually became obsolete. Photocopying has improved the quality and the number of reproductions that can be run from an original document. Manual typewriters are now also considered antiques. Today, computers and printers can do the job with way less time and effort. The delete button on the keyboard makes correcting errors a snap.

It is easy to tell those who haven't typed much since their high school days, because they seem to have forgotten where the keys are located. Even on a fast computer, they are in the hunt and peck mode. I, on the other hand, enjoy getting into a rhythm and hearing the keyboard go clickety, clack. Still, it pales in comparison to the musical **DING** of the old manual typewriter. Some sounds just don't seem to get outdated.

43
The Famous Musical Gate

My older sister Delores, our mutual friend Sheri and I were working gals, and each of us had earned another two weeks of vacation time. We had taken several trips together in the past by flying to Hawaii, Mexico and Las Vegas. This time we wanted to go on a long, leisurely drive across the United States. Delores had just bought herself a new car, and she was willing to take it on the trip. Before we set out, the three of us agreed that we didn't want to be held down to exact travel plans. Instead, we hoped for some adventure and to see some interesting sites along the way.

Our journey began on a lovely May morning in 1975 in northeastern Colorado. We traveled through Kansas and Missouri before deciding to head south. We saw parts of Arkansas and eventually ended up in Nashville, Tennessee.

Being young, single women, we certainly knew that Elvis lived in Nashville. We did a little investigating, found out where Graceland was located and decided to drive by. As we traveled down Elvis Presley Boulevard, we didn't get a good view of the famous singer's property. We did, however, notice the ornate gate at the entrance of his driveway. Sheri suggested that it would make a neat picture with us standing in front of it. That's when our adventuresome side came out. We drove approximately a half mile, spotted a parking lot and pulled in. The only problem was we were now on the opposite side of the highway from where the mansion was located. But as luck would have it, we had accidentally stumbled onto a store that sold Elvis memorabilia. After going inside and purchasing some souvenirs, we were ready to make a daring attempt to cross the busy highway.

The three of us waited patiently for a good opening before taking off sprinting. We ran as if our lives depended upon it. Just to make sure that we were out of harm's way we continued to dash across the sidewalk, down a grassy embankment to the bottom of a ditch. Our reactions were instantaneous and unanimous. We squealed, but not because we saw Elvis. Much to our surprise, we were sinking into a thick layer of mud.

We gathered our composure and clumsily climbed back up the embankment to the sidewalk. It wasn't good! Our sandals were covered with stinky muck as were the lower portions of our bell-bottoms. As farmers' daughters we were used to getting muddy while helping our fathers irrigate, but this was different. We were all dressed up and our hotel room was miles away. Even though we were embarrassed by our appearance, we weren't about to give up on our idea of posing in front of Elvis's gate. Especially since, we were so close and would probably never be in the vicinity again.

Definitely feeling like three country girls with squishy, muddy feet, we began walking alongside the bustling city traffic. We wondered what people driving by were thinking. But our biggest concern was whether the splattered mud on our bell-bottoms would show up on our Polaroid photos or not.

After reaching the legendary singer's cement driveway, we were in awe. The famous gate, which was there to keep fans like us off of Elvis's property, was gracefully designed. Fittingly, decorations in the shape of musical notes adorned it. On the two sides of the gate, exquisitely formed metal looked like Elvis playing his guitar.

We began taking pictures and weren't quite finished with our photography session when a long, black limousine pulled off of the highway. We quickly stepped aside. The expression on our faces probably showed how astonished and humiliated we were feeling at that moment. We couldn't see in the windows, for they were tinted a dark black. Secretly, each of us was wondering, "Is Elvis in that chauffeur-driven car?" We were too stunned to even wave. The big gate split in two, opened wide and the luxurious limousine pulled through it. We just stood there and watched the event happen. Of course, the gate was quickly closed for security reasons.

Delores, Sheri and I didn't know if Elvis saw us, but we were hoping he did. If he was actually inside the limousine, he probably wondered why three country-looking girls were hanging around his gate with mud on their bell-bottoms. He might have even thought we looked a little crazy. Then again, the rock 'n roll star was used to his fans acting rather outlandish. So maybe not!

As we walked back to our car, we giggled about our unexpected experience at the famous musical gate. The three of us really were on the kind of vacation we had planned, and we had good pictures to prove it.

44
By the Bushel Basket

As I recall, we had two specific uses for our sturdy, wooden bushel baskets. Whenever we went apple picking at a nearby orchard, we took several of them along to hold the bounty of a good harvest. Mom also used one of them as her laundry basket for years. It had a cloth lining, which had a couple of slits that fit over the wire handles.

While Dad wasn't responsible for doing the washing or hanging it out on the clotheslines to dry, I recall how he did "hamper" Mom's effort on one occasion. It went something like this: The wind wasn't blowing hard, and it was coming from the right direction to burn a few irrigation ditches. So on an early Monday afternoon, he tossed a lit match onto a pile of dry tumbleweeds. He stuck around to make sure the blaze didn't get out of hand. He'd gotten caught one time before while burning ditches. The fire got away from him, went roaring down our pasture and

Laundry hanging out on the clothesline to dry was a common sight around our home. The wooden bushel basket pictured is one that survived from our farming days.

made its way over to the neighbor's place before he got it stopped. Fortunately, the conditions were perfect this time.

The smell of weed smoke filtering in through the open windows is what got Mom's attention. She hurried outside, saw the source and immediately knew who was responsible for it. "He could have said something about wanting to burn ditches when we ate dinner!" she complained as she quickly grabbed her empty clothes basket. She began stripping the lines at a furious pace. Back in the house, she was still muttering, "I can't read his mind. If I knew that's what he was going to do, I would have gotten my clothes in earlier. They were dry anyway."

Hours later, when the fire died out, Dad came home. Mom emphatically told him that she had clothes out on the line when he started burning. "I didn't know that," he said sheepishly.

"Well, it's Monday!" she exclaimed. "That's the day I always wash!"

For many years, Mom only washed one day per week. As long as the weather cooperated, Monday was her official laundry day. During my early childhood years, I recall her using a wringer washer. A large tub of water was heated up on the stove, and then dumped into the washer where the clothes were agitated. When it had finished washing, she fed the soapy garments through the tension-set rollers of the wringer. She had to be very careful not to get her fingers caught in it. The wrung-out clothes fell into a tub of rinse water. She then pivoted the wringer and ran the garments through the rollers and into her laundry basket. She was able to use the same water for six or so loads by washing the whites first and our jeans last. After the last load was done, she attached another hose onto the washer and drained the dirty, soapy water out into the yard.

Later, she upgraded to an automatic washing machine that had a suds saver option. Once again, she was able to use the same soap and water for multiple loads. Near her washer was a two-sided holding basin that was about three feet tall. The soapy water drained into one portion of the tin container, while the other side was used to hold the rinse water. The washer had a pump, which returned the water that was needed in the current cycle.

Back in those days, Mom added bluing to the rinse water to help whiten the whites. She also starched our shirts, blouses, dresses, dresser scarves, etc. She purchased starch by the box and added the white powder to cold water. After the starch was dissolved, she immersed the wet, just washed items into the starch water. She wrung them out with her hands and hung them on the line to dry. They would be ironed later.

By late morning, the heavy-duty clothesline wires were

drooping under the weight of the wet clothes. When the wind came along, it would lift and whip them about. The sheets and pillowcases quickly dried and became as lively as sails on a boat. Although Mom had an automatic dryer, she rarely used it except when the weather was terrible. She preferred hanging everything outdoors to dry naturally, thus saving on electricity.

In the afternoon, the clothes were taken off the lines and hauled back indoors. Folding was done and beds were made. Mom separated out all the items she'd be ironing the next day and put them on the kitchen table. The plastic bottle she used to sprinkle clothes with had a lid with tiny holes in it. After everything was sprinkled, rolled up and placed in the wooden bushel basket, she folded the cloth lining over them so they'd stay damp.

On Tuesday morning, Mom spent a lot of time at her ironing board. As she pressed the starched garments, it restored their newness by giving the clothing a crisp, semistiff appearance and more body. Before she hung up Dad's dress shirt, she routinely tucked money into his pocket for the following Sunday's collection basket. That way she wouldn't forget to do so.

As the size of our family grew, Mom added a second wash day. Then her standard schedule was to do laundry on Mondays and Fridays. While she was in charge of washing clothes by the bushel basket, that same measurement meant something entirely different to Dad. He was concerned with how many bushels per acre the corn, pinto beans, oats and barley he was raising was producing. Laundry or crops, those bushels really added up to be "tons of work" for both of them. But, then again, that's what vintage, small farm life was like.

Bushels of Memories

In the hustle and bustle
Throughout a day,
Lots of things happen
Along the way.

Into a basket
Items get tossed,
With the hope
They don't get lost.

Life keeps on moving,
More gets dropped in;
Without knowing it,
You've got a full bin.

Memories get picked
Out of the blue,
To think about
Like they're brand new.